APPLIED ENGLISH PHONOLOGY

For ESL/EFL Teachers

Raja T. Nasr

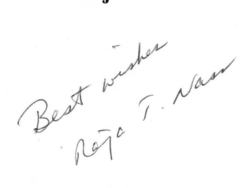

Best wishes
Raja T. Nasr

University Press of America, Inc.
Lanham • New York • Oxford

Copyright © 1997 by
University Press of America,® Inc.
4720 Boston Way
Lanham, Maryland 20706

12 Hid's Copse Rd.
Cummor Hill, Oxford OX2 9JJ

Library of Congress Cataloging-in-Publication Data

Nasr, Raja Tewfik
Applied English phonology : for ESL/EFL teachers / Raja T. Nasr.
p.   cm.
Includes bibliographical references and index.
1. English language--Study and teaching--Foreign speakers. 2.
English language--Phonology. I. Title.
PE1128.A2N33   1997   428'.007--dc21   96-48662 CIP

ISBN 0-7618-0640-7 (cloth: alk. ppr.)
ISBN 0-7618-0641-5 (pbk: alk. ppr.)

This book is dedicated

to the memory of

Robert Lado

with gratitude

Table of Contents

Preface

Linguistic science has developed very rapidly in the last fifty years. Books on the subject number by the hundreds. Courses in linguistic science are very common in colleges and universities. Students of language and literature are now required to take a variety of courses in theoretical and applied linguistics. Even students in such fields as sociology, education, and anthropology are advised (and, in some cases, required) to take courses in linguistics because of the interrelationship that exists among these areas of study.

Linguistic science has also influenced language textbooks. No language book is considered to be of any value if it is not based on some of the findings of modern linguistics. This and other factors have also influenced teacher training programs. No language teacher (and especially no second or foreign language teacher) can escape linguistic science if she/he expects to do her/his job effectively and on a scientific basis.

My experience with foreign language teachers (especially teachers of English as a second or foreign language) in many parts of the world (primarily in the Middle East, North and East Africa, Europe, the UK, and the USA) has clearly indicated the dire need for presenting, in a simple and direct fashion, the basic principles and practices of the various branches of applied linguistics.

Applied English Phonology: for ESL/EFL Teachers is an attempt at meeting a part of this great need. This book is meant to help teachers of English give speakers of other languages the basic information and tools they need to help their students master the phonological system of English and overcome some of the more serious problems they face in doing so. The elements emphasized are those that contribute to more effective classroom practices.

More specifically, teachers of English as a second or foreign language should find this book of value to them in a number of ways: as a tool to sharpen their own ears to hear some sounds (in English and other languages) that they might not have heard or been aware of before; as a tool to help them pronounce English sounds more intelligibly and accurately; as a resource on the phonological system of English; as a contributing factor to more effective linguistic pedagogy in the classroom; and as a way to the development of a more wholesome attitude towards language, all aspects of language teaching and learning in general, and towards pronunciation in particular.

A glossary of technical terms is found at the end of the book to help teachers understand the jargon in the field. For those who are interested in pursuing more in-depth information in the field of phonology, a selected bibliography is given. Also of help, especially for review purposes, is the list of study questions.

Raja T. Nasr
Alexandria, Virginia, 1996

Chapter One

The Place of Phonology in Language Study

1. What is Language?

Language is a part of culture; it is a part of human behavior. Language is an acquired set of habits of systematic vocal activity representing meanings derived from human experiences. One can also say, simply, that language is an acquired vocal system for communicating meanings. This statement implies:

- (a) that language operates in a regular and systematic fashion,
- (b) that language is basically oral, and that the oral symbols represent meanings as they are related to real life situations and experiences, and
- (c) that language has a social function, and that without it society would probably not exist.

2. What is Correct Language?

Since language is a part of culture and also a part of human behavior, our attitude towards it must not be different from that towards any other part of culture or human behavior. Any act in our social life - such as the kind of clothes we wear, the table manners we use, the subjects we talk about, and so on - would be either correct or incorrect depending on the situation in which the act is performed. An evening function may require a special kind of dress; a dinner invitation may require a different table setting; and the subjects for discussion will vary in business meetings or friendly gatherings. Such too is the case with language.

The development of London English as the Standard Dialect in the fourteenth and fifteenth centuries was due basically to the importance of London as the center of major activities - social, economic, educational, and political. People in different parts of England, wanting to be like the people in important positions, learned London English, sometimes very much as a second language or dialect. In the United States of America a standard dialect developed in much the same way as in England. And today any person growing up in an area that uses a different dialect learns Standard American English, also very much as a second language or dialect.

There are as many 'Englishes' in the world as there are native speakers of English; and Standard English in England and in the United States of America is made up of the common features of pronunciation, vocabulary, and grammar as they are used by educated people in important positions. Standard English changes to the extent that these people change the common features of their speech.

It is *not* the way we think those people *ought* to speak that determines the Standard dialect; it is, rather, the way they actually *do* speak that determines it.

What is correct or incorrect in a language at any given time is determined only on the basis of how educated people in important positions actually *use* the language.

3. The Component Parts of Language

Language, as a system, operates in set patterns. These patterns exist on three closely related levels - phonology, vocabulary, and grammar. Another way of saying this is to consider the component parts of language as phonology, morphology, and syntax. However, since the focal point of this book is phonology, the differences in the two ways we refer to the component parts of language need not be of major concern here.

Phonology. The features of sound in a language are systematically structured. They are divided into two main branches:

(a) the branch of segmental features including
    consonants and vowels, and
(b) the branch of supra-segmental features including
    stress, intonation, pause, juncture, and rhythm.

Vocabulary. The vocabulary of a language consists of the lexical forms (words) that refer to parts of our experience. In English, these words consist of consonants and vowels arranged in special sequences.

Grammar. Grammar consists of the means by which relationships between words are shown. These relationships also come from our experiences. The means by which relationships are shown include:

> (a) inflection, which is the changes in the forms of words (such as *cat/cats, like/liked, big/bigger, etc.*),
> (b) word order, which is the arrangement of words in relation to each other (as in *He is here./Is he here?*) and
> (c) grammatical words, which in themselves signal grammatical relationships without having any lexical meaning (such as *shall, could, of, at,* etc.). The features of grammar, like the features of sound, are systematically structured in patterns.

4. The Place of Phonology in Language Study

As is stated above, phonology is a part of language; it is a basic component part of language. Phonology is unique in its role as a component part of language, because it permeates both the vocabulary and the grammar of a language. It is an essential element in all utterances.

Chapter Two

Phonetics

1. What is Phonetics?

Phonetics is the study of speech sounds or *phones*. It is important to remember that phonetics deals with speech sounds as a recording machine would receive them or as they hit human ear drums before they are interpreted. In other words, phonetics is the study of speech sounds *objectively*.

Human ears need to be sharpened in order to *hear* sounds objectively. Sharp ears would be able to distinguish two different speech sounds even if the difference between them is very minute. For example, it takes some training or sharpening of the ears to hear the difference between the two "p" sounds in "pat" and "spat". If you are a native speaker of English, you would normally produce the "p" in "pat" with much more of a puff of air than with the "p" in "spat". Phonetically, these two words would be written this way:

[p^{h}æt] "pat"
[spæt] "spat"

Square brackets indicate that the sounds are written phonetically. *Double quotation marks* are used around words spelled *orthographically*.

Phonetics, of course, is not limited to the use of phonetic symbols in the transcription of sounds. *Articulatory phonetics* also includes the preparation of *phonetic charts* and the *phonetic description* of speech sounds. The phonetic description of speech sounds covers both the *points of articulation* and the *types of articulation* in the production of speech sounds. *Auditory phonetics* deals with the way speech sounds are heard through the physiological organs of hearing. *Acoustic phonetics* deals with the sound waves going through the air.

2. Basic Sound Production

No speech sounds can be produced without having some air involved either going out (as in exhaling) or going in (as in inhaling). In the vast majority of speech sound productions, the air goes out. When sounds are produced with the air going out, the sounds are called *egressive sounds*. When they are produced with the air going in, they are called *ingressive sounds*.

There are seven openings in the human head: two eyes, two ears, two nostrils (the nose), and one mouth. In speech production, the air goes either through the mouth, making *oral sounds*, or through the nose, making *nasal sounds*.

If the air goes out rather freely through the mouth or through the nose, very little sound, if any, is heard. In speech production, the air coming out makes sounds if the air is stopped somewhere and then released or if it rubs against some surface or surfaces causing friction. In other words, it is some sort of interruption of the free flow of air (within the vocal apparatus) that results in speech sounds.

Diagram of the vocal apparatus <u>Parts of the Apparatus</u>

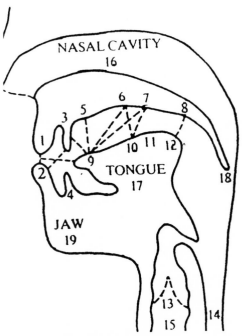

1. Upper lip
2. Lower lip
3. Upper teeth
4. Lower teeth
5. Tooth ridge
   (Alveolar ridge)
6. Hard palate
7. Palate
8. Velum(Soft palate)
9. Tongue tip
10. Tongue front or blade
11. Tongue middle
12. Tongue back
13. Vocal cords(Voice box)
14. Food passage
15. Air passage
16. Nasal cavity
17. Tongue
18. Uvula
19. Jaw

3. The Vocal Apparatus

Practically all diagrams of the vocal apparatus have the front of the face turned towards the left or the west. Study the diagram well and learn to name its parts. Also practice drawing the vocal apparatus yourself. Start from the left and do the upper part first. Then start again from the left and do the lower part. Put in the vocal cords last.

4. The Speech Organs

To get a better grasp of the speech organs, it would be helpful to refer to the diagram of the vocal apparatus in the preceding section. Acquaintance with the speech organs and the role they play in speech production can be highly instrumental not only in acquiring the ability to produce different speech sounds, but also in helping learners acquire the same ability.

Starting with the front of the mouth and moving backwards, the speech organs are the following:

a. The lips.

The upper lip and the lower lip are used in a variety of ways to produce sounds. For example, the sound [p] is produced by having the air stopped at the lips before it is released. When both lips are used in the production of sounds, the sounds are called *bilabial* sounds. The shape of the lips is also important in the production of sounds. Notice, for example, the different shapes of the lips in the production of the vowels in the following words:

"pool" (rounded lips)
"peel" (spread out lips)
"pal" (rather wide open lips).

b.   The teeth.
The upper front teeth and the lower front teeth are, unlike the lips, not movable, but they are used in the production of certain sounds. In some languages (for example, Arabic, Greek, and Italian) most speakers have the tip of the tongue touch the back of the upper front teeth producing the sounds [t] and [d]. When this happens, the sounds are called *dental* sounds.

In the production of some sounds like [θ] (the "th" in "thin") and [ʃ] (the "th" in "then"), the tongue tip goes somewhere between the upper and lower front teeth as the air goes out of the mouth. When this happens, the sounds are called *inter-dental* sounds. In the speech of some speakers, these two sounds, [θ] and [ʃ], are produced by having the tongue tip go very close to the back of the upper front teeth. With still other speakers, the tongue tip can be clearly seen protruding between the upper and lower front teeth.

c. Lip and teeth.
Some sounds, like [f] and [v], are produced by having the upper front teeth come very close to (almost to the point of touching) the lower lip. Such sounds are called *labio-dental* sounds.

d. The alveolar ridge.
This is sometimes called the *tooth ridge* or the *teeth ridge*. If you use your tongue tip to sweep backwards, starting with the lower part of your upper front teeth, you will notice a lump or ridge immediately behind the top part of the upper front teeth. This is the *alveolar ridge* and it is used in the production of sounds by having the tongue tip touch it or come very close to it. For example:

[t] and [d] as produced by most Americans and
[l] as in "let" and "low".

e. The hard palate.

This is the part of the roof of the mouth just back of the alveolar ridge. You can feel the hardness with your tongue tip. While the hard palate is not movable, the tongue can touch it or come close to it in producing certain sounds. When the very front part of this hard palate is used in the production of such sounds as [ʃ] (as in "s̲hine" and [ʒ] (as in "mea̲sure"), the sounds are called *alveo-palatal* sounds. When the back part of the hard palate is used in the production of such sounds as [j] (as in "y̲oung"), the sounds are called *palatal* sounds.

f. The velum.

This is sometimes referred to as the *soft palate.* When a part of the tongue mid or tongue back moves up to touch or to come close to the velum or soft palate, the sounds produced are called *velar* sounds. Examples of such sounds are [k] as in "c̲oal" and [g] as in "g̲oal".

g. The uvula.

This is a movable part at the far back of the roof of the mouth. When this uvula drops down to touch the back part of the tongue (which actually goes up to meet it), the sounds produced are very much like a very far backed [k]. Arabic is an example of a language that uses such a *uvular* sound.

h. The glottis.

This is the part of the vocal apparatus that is way back in the throat. Lying at that point are the vocal cords.

i. The vocal cords.

These are two muscular membranes that resemble a set of two curtains drawn away from each other. When the vocal cords are drawn apart, the air flows freely in and out of the mouth. If they happen to shut off the air temporarily before the air is released, the sound produced is a *glottal* sound. An English utterance beginning with a vowel is usually produced with an initial glottal stop. Some languages, such as Arabic, use the glottal stop in a variety of positions.

The vocal cords are also used to produce two major varieties of sound quality. When, in the production of speech sounds, the vocal cords vibrate, the sounds are called *voiced* sounds. When, in the production of speech sounds, the vocal cords do not vibrate (or when the vibration is minimal), the sounds are called *voiceless* or *unvoiced* sounds. [z], [v], [b], and [a] are examples of voiced sounds. [s], [f], [p] and [t] are examples of voiceless sounds.

j. The tongue.
The tongue is a very significant, and movable, part of the vocal apparatus or speech organs. Four relative parts of the tongue help in producing different speech sounds. These are:

- the *tongue tip* (used in producing [t], [d], and [l]),
- the *tongue front* or *blade* (used in producing [s] and [z]),
- the *tongue middle* or *mid* (used in producing [j]), and
- the *tongue back* (used in producing [k] and [g]).

Additionally, the tongue moves to take a variety of shapes and positions in the mouth to produce different speech sounds. Use a small mirror to see (or try to feel) the various shapes and positions of the tongue in the production of different vowels in the following words: "beet", "bit", "bait", "bet", "bat", "but", "pool", "pull", "pole", and "Paul". Notice how the tongue moves from one position to another in the mouth when producing the vowels in the following words: "buy", "bough", and "boy".

k. The nose.
While the nose itself is in the front of the face, the *nasal passage* actually extends all the way from the front of the face to the very back of the vocal apparatus. In the production of some speech sounds, the air is blocked in the mouth and allowed to go out through the nasal passage. Examples of such sounds are [m] and [n], which would be called *nasal* sounds. In the speech of some people (as in the case of a good number of Americans), the vowels preceding and following nasal consonants have some air also going through the nose or nasal passage. Such vowels would be called *nasalized* sounds.

l. The jaw.
The lower jaw is the part of the head that moves. The relative openness or closure of the jaw helps to produce various sound qualities. Notice, for example, the relative openness of the jaw in producing the vowels in the following words: "bit", "bet", and "bat".

Chapter Three

The Production of Speech Sounds

1. Introduction

As has been mentioned earlier, it is the interruption of the free flow of air through the vocal apparatus that causes speech sounds to be produced. The nature of this interruption determines the type of sound produced. For example, if the nature of the interruption is a temporary stoppage of the air before it is allowed to go out, the sound would be a *stop*; sometimes *stops* are called *plosives*. If, for another example, the interruption is not a full stoppage (or blockage) of the air, but some sort of constriction that makes the air rub against some surfaces in the vocal apparatus, then the sound would be a *fricative*, referring to the friction that the air causes. [t], [d], [k], and [g] are examples of *stops*; [s], [z], [f], and [v] are examples of *fricatives*.

In the ensuing sections, various *types* of sound articulation are explained, and various *points* of sound articulation are presented in a slightly different way from the explanation of the parts of the speech organs presented earlier. A thorough understanding of the *types* and *points* of articulation can be very instrumental not only in your own production of speech sounds, but also in helping ESL/EFL learners produce the sounds of English that may present some problems for them.

2. The Types of Sound Articulation

The following types of sound articulation are among the most common:

(a) *Stops* or *Plosives*. These are sounds which are produced by stopping the air somewhere in the mouth or vocal passage and then releasing it. The word *stop* refers to the stopping of the air; the word *plosive* refers to the release of the air. Two of the stops in English are:

[p] (voiceless; that is with the vocal cords not vibrating)

[b] (voiced; that is with the vocal cords vibrating)

(The opposite of a stop is a *continuant,* which can last or continue longer.)

(b) *Fricatives* or *Sibilants*. These are sounds which are produced by having the air rub against some surface in the mouth or vocal passage, causing friction. Two of the fricatives in English are:

[s] (voiceless)

[z] (voiced)

(c) *Affricates*. These are sounds which are made up of two parts: a stop and a fricative. The two English affricates are:

[tʃ] (voiceless)

[dʒ] (voiced)

(d) *Nasals*. These are sounds which are produced with the air going through the nose or nasal cavity. Two of the English nasals are:

[m] (voiced)

[n] (voiced)

(e) *Laterals*. These are sounds which are produced by having the air go out of the mouth from both sides of the tongue. The only English lateral is:

[l] (voiced)

(f) *Vibrants*. These are sounds which are produced by having the tongue vibrate in the mouth. The only English vibrant is:

[r] (voiced)

(g) *Semi-vowels*. These are sounds which are considered half consonants and half vowels. They are like consonants in their structural behavior; and they are like vowels in their quality. The English semi-vowels are:

[w] (voiced)

[j] (voiced)

3. Voiced and Voiceless Speech Sounds

When the vocal cords vibrate, they cause voicing. Any sound produced with the vocal cords vibrating is called a *voiced* sound. When the vocal cords do not vibrate (actually in speech they always vibrate, but here the vibration is very little), the sound is called a *voiceless* sound.

There are two easy ways to feel or discover the vibration of the vocal cords:

  (a) Put two or three fingers on your Adam's apple and say [s]; you will feel little or no vibration. Now keep your fingers in the same place and say [z]; you will feel much more vibration.

  (b) Cover your ears with the palms of your hands and say [s]; you will feel and hear little or no vibration. Now keep the palms of your hands on your ears and say [z]; you will feel and hear much more vibration.

All the vowels in English and most of the consonants are voiced. It is only when we whisper that all the consonants and vowels become voiceless.

4. The Points of Sound Articulation

The types of sounds discussed above are produced at different points in the vocal passage. The diagram of the vocal apparatus (shown earlier) has all the parts of the apparatus with different numbers given to them. Study the diagram very well and become familiar with the names of the various parts of the vocal apparatus. In explaining and naming the different points of articulation, the same numbers are used as in the diagram. Refer to the diagram constantly as you learn the new names of the points of articulation.

The following points of articulation are among the most common (with examples in English, unless otherwise mentioned):

  (a) *Bilabial* (1,2). When the point of articulation is at the upper and lower lips, the sound is bilabial.
  Examples: [p] (voiceless); [b] (voiced); [m] (voiced nasal).

  (b) *Labio-dental* (2,3). When the point of articulation is at the upper set of teeth and the lower lip, the sound is labio-dental.
  Examples: [f] (voiceless); [v] (voiced).

  (c) *Inter-dental* (9,3,4). When the point of articulation is the tongue tip between the upper and lower teeth (or at least very near the teeth, especially the upper set), the sound is interdental.

Examples: [θ] (voiceless) "thing"; [ð] (voiced) "then."

(d)   *Dental* (9,3). When the point of articulation is at the tongue tip and the inside of the upper front teeth, the sound is dental.

Examples: Arabic and French [t] (voiceless) and [d] (voiced).

(e)   *Alveolar* (9,5). When the point of articulation is at the tongue tip and the alveolar ridge, the sound is alveolar.

Examples: [n] (voiced nasal); [l] (voiced lateral); [s] (voiceless); and English [t] (voiceless) and [d] voiced.

(f)   *Retroflex* (9,7). When the point of articulation is at the tongue when it is turned back into the mouth under the palate, the sound is a retroflex sound.

Example: American English [r] (voiced vibrant).

(g)   *Alveo-palatal* (10,6). When the point of articulation is at the tongue front (or middle) and the hard palate, the sound is alveo-palatal.

Examples: [ʃ] (voiceless); [ʒ] (voiced).

(h)   *Palatal* (11,7). When the point of articulation is at the tongue middle and the palate, the sound is palatal.

Example: [j] (voiced semi-vowel).

(i)   *Velar* (12,8). When the point of articulation is at the tongue back and the velum (soft palate), the sound is velar.

Examples: [k] (voiceless); [g] (voiced).

(j)   *Uvular* (12,18). When the point of articulation is at the tongue back and the uvula, the sound is uvular.

Example: Arabic [q] (voiceless).

(k)   *Glottal.* When the point of articulation is at the glottis (in the throat), the sound is glottal.

Examples: [h] (voiceless); [ʔ] (voiceless), which is used in many languages (such as Arabic) as a consonant phoneme.

Chapter Four

Phonetic Exercises

1. Introduction

The main purpose of this chapter is to give teachers of English as a second or foreign language a vehicle by which they can sharpen their ears (i.e. be able to hear a variety of sounds) and have greater control over the production of speech sounds, especially ones that do not occur normally in English speech. Perhaps a secondary objective is for teachers of English to realize that, while the production of "foreign" sounds may seem difficult, knowledge about articulatory phonetics can be a great aid in manipulating the various parts of the speech organs to produce the desired sounds.

Towards these ends, sample exercises are given for the production of a variety of types of sound articulation at different points of articulation. The phonetic description of the sounds and the occasional hints given about their production should be helpful.

2. Stops

a. (When a sound is aspirated, make sure there is enough of a puff of air to help blow out a candle.)
    Produce the following phonetic utterances with or without aspiration as indicated in the phonetic transcription: [pʰæli:].

[pæli:], [kru:pʰ], [papʰ], [lepə], [li:pʰu:], [pʰaipər], [paipʰər], [su:pʰ], [su:p].

unrealeased

Produce the following utterances with alveolar [t] sounds: [tʰi:p], [peitʰ], [spu:t], [steik], [kʰeitu:], [sæti], [tʰau], [tou], [wat], [ki:tʰ].
Produce the same utterances above, making the [t] sounds dental. (Make sure your tongue tip touches the back of the upper front teeth.)

b. *Voiced and Voiceless Stops*
Produce the followong utterances and say which stops are dental and which are alveolar: [bu:dei], [kʰoudit], [di:bæl], [gu:kʰei], [gæbi:], [dougætʰ]. [bi:du], [gri:kou], [seikʰu:n], [dæti:kou].

c. *Other Stops*
(1) You already know that the vowels in the words "keen", "coat", and "call" move the point of articulation of [k] progressively backwards. Now try to produce the same English words, each time making the [k] sound in each word take different articulatory positions.
(2) Produce a uvular [k] by having your tongue back touch the uvula for a stop. With that point of articulation, produce the following: [kan], [ku:], [kei], [ki:], [lak], bi:k], [laku], [liki].
(3) Produce a glottal stop [ʔ] audibly be saying the words "I", "oh", "eel", "out", "oil". Now produce these utterances: [ʔani:], [ʔæni:], [lu:ʔ], [si:ʔu], [bi:ʔ], [miʔeit], [bu:ʔi:], [siʔ].

3. **Fricatives**
a. Produce the following utterances and say which fricatives are voiced and which are voiceless: [fiʃ], [væʃi:], [mu:ʒ], [mauʒif], [si:ʃæv], [fu:ziθ], [ʃæʃ], [θauʃou], [maʃaθ], [zi:pʰeθ].
b. *Bilabial Fricatives*
Instead of saying [f], let both lips come close together so that the friction is bilabial: a voiceless bilabial fricative [ɸ]. Now say [ɸei], [ɸui], [ouɸ].
Now make the same sound with the vocal cords vibrating: a voiced bilabial fricative [β]. Say [βe:], [βu:], [ouβ].

Now produce them in pairs: [ɸei]: [bei], [ɸuː]: [buː], and [ouɸ]:[oub].

c. *Other Fricatives*

trilled – untrilled [x] is a voiceless velar fricative. Say [xan], [lax], [xuːd], [maxi], [luːxa], [siːxal].

[ɣ] is a voiced velar fricative. Say [ɣuːli], [suːɣa], [buːɣ], [luːɣa], [ɣaniː], [miɣ].

[ħ] is a voiceless pharyngeal fricative. Say [ħuːt], [siːħa], [nuːħ], [pæħ], [ħiːna].

[9] is a voiced pharyngeal fricative. Say [9uːm], [9aluː], [læ9], [siː9a], [ʃæ9], [laː9uː].

4. Affricates

a. Say the following English words. Then transcribe them phonetically and say which affricates are voiceless and which are voiced and what their points of articulation are: "chop", "match", "just", "matching", "fudge", "catch", "judge", "major".

b. *Other Affricates*
Produce these utterances: [tsiːkuː], [matsuː], [dzuːki], [miːdzuː], [bakʃiː], [luːgʒa].

5. Laterals

Hear the difference between the two [l] sounds in "let" and "tell" and in "lit" and "tall". The [l] in "lit" and "let" is lighter than the [l] in "tall" and "tell". (In the latter words, the [l] is darker.) Produce the following words twice each, once with a light [l] and then with a dark [l]: "play", "lease", "pal", "tall", "fellow", "follow", "feeling", "will", "alloy", "fly".

Whether the [l] is light or dark, the air goes out of the mouth on both sides of the tongue. That is why the sound is called lateral. Now produce these English words by causing some friction as the air goes out on both sides of the tongue (a voiceless fricative [ɬ]): [ɬi], [baɬ], [fiːluː].

6. Vibrants

A retroflexed [r] is one produced with the tongue tip curled back as in the words "run" and "rain". A flapped [r] is produced by having the tongue tip flap once against the alveolar ridge. A trilled [r] is produced by having the tongue tip flap two or (usually) three times against the alveolar ridge. All three, of course, are voiced. Now produce the following English words three times each: first with a retroflexed [r], then with a flapped [r], and finally with a trilled [r]:   "run", "rain", "far", "star", "stir", "marry", "fortune", "bark", "ferry", "prune", "startle", "breakfast".

Hear the difference between the [r] in "rain" and the [r] in "train" in your own speech. Because of the [t] in "train", you might notice something of a fricative [r] in the word "train". If you have heard it, try to say the following words with a fricative [r]:   "troop", "trill", "rule", "rain", "merry", "attract", "drape", "creep".

7. Nasals

The nasal consonants in English are /m n ŋ/. In American English, the vowels before and after nasal consonants tend usually to be nasalizes as well. See if you can hear more nasalization in your own speech when you say the second sentence as compared with the first:

(1) I sat with a fellow worker to discuss salaries.

(2) My morning plane landed on time in Maine.

Now try to say the first sentence with considerable nasalization (i.e. by having some air go out continuously through your nose). Now try the second sentence without nasalizing any of the vowels (i.e. by making all the vowels oral rather than nasal).

8. Vowels and Vocoids

You know that the [i:] in "seat" is fronted and produced with the lips stretched out (unrounded). The [u:] in "pool" is backed and produced with rounded lips. Now say a long [i:] and, as you are producing it, keep your tongue in the same fronted position in the mouth and progressively move your lips to a rounded position. This should give you a sound that is significant in French.

Now do the opposite. Produce a long [u:] and, as you are doing that, keep your tongue in the same backed position in the mouth and progressively move your lips to a stretched out position. This should give you a sound that is significant in a number of languages. In both cases, a small mirror might help you see what you are doing with your lips.

In your own speech, you might notice a glide in the vowels in these words: "say" and "so". The vowels actually go from [e] to [i] in "say" and from [o] to [u] in "so". Now try to say these same words without the glide, i.e. without going to the second element of the vowel. For further practice, try to say the following words without glides and with the first element of the vowels made slightly longer: "late", "fail", "play", "main", "dame", "coat", "moan", "row", "own", "sole". Several English dialects (e.g. Irish and Scottish) have such vowels.

9. Phonetic Transcription

a.   Listen to yourself, or better still, record your own voice as you read parts of the Preface in this book. Now transcribe phonetically what you hear, including any small variations of sounds.

b.   Record a few utterances spoken in another language by a native speaker of that language. Then transcribe what you hear phonetically.

c.   Write two or three sentences in class and let different members of your class read them. Transcribe phonetically what you hear, indicating any particular differences in the various speeches.

(When different persons transcribe what they hear spoken by the same person, do not be shocked at the differences in the transcriptions; marvel at the similarities.)

Chapter Five

Phonemics

1. What is Phonemics?

Phonemics is the study of the *phonological system* of a particular language. From this point of view, phonemics is a *relative* study. Each language would have its own phonological system. The word *system* in the definition of *phonemics* refers to the way the various sounds (or phones) of a language are organized or structured or patterned in contrastive units or bundles or phonemes.

Phonetics may be considered the starting point or the basis for *phonemics*. In other words, phonetics is a part of phonemics; to do phonemics, one must deal with phonetics. The opposite is not true. The study of phonetics need not proceed to phonemics.

While *phonetics* deals with speech sounds as they are produced or as they are heard (objectively) or as they travel in waves through the air, *phonemics* deals with how human speech sounds are *perceived* or *interpreted* once they are heard. This perception or interpretation is essentially neuro-psychological, and it is developed and formed at a very young age. Usually by the age of two or two and a half years the phonemic system is well established neuro-psychologically in children.

2. The Phoneme

Let us start with an analogy to clarify a notion. The notion to be clarified is *contrastiveness*. The United nations has delegates representing the various member states. Among the delegates is one representing the United States of America. Now the U.S.A. has a population of about 250,000,000 people. Any one of these can legitimately represent the U.S.A. *In the context of the U.N.*, it makes *no* difference who represents the U.S.A. Any of the 250,000,000 citizens could do it. In other words, *in the context of the U.N., the various (250,000,000) U.S. citizens are not in contrast with each other.*

The U.N., of course, has representatives of other countries. The same principle stated above applies to all other countries represented in the U.N. If Country X has a population of 80,000,000 citizens, any one of those citizens may be designated to represent Country X. Again, *in the context of the U.N., the various (80,000,000) citizens of Country X are not in contrast with each other.*

However, *in the context of the U.N., any individual of the 250,000,000 citizens of the U.S. would be in contrast with any individual of the 80,000,000 citizens of country X.* This is so because the individuals referred to would be representing *different* countries. *In the context of the U.N., it is these different countries that are contrastive with each other.*

Applying the principles of this analogy to phonology should be very easy. Instead of dealing with the context of the U.N., in phonology the context would be one particular language at a time. In any one language, there are hundreds of sounds (or phones) that can be heard and described by a phonetician. The phones are absolute; they are universal. A description of a phone will apply everywhere. For example, a voiceless unaspirated bilabial stop would be represented phonetically as [p]. (All phones are phonetic sounds.) This [p] may exist in several languages. But in each language it will be analyzed differently. In some languages it may be a significant sound, and in some other languages, it may be an insignificant sound. To use some words of the analogy, this [p] may represent a contrastive sound unit in a particular language, while in some other languages it may be one of several non-contrastive varieties within a sound unit or bundle that is contrastive with other sound units or bundles.

The phones of a particular language form themselves into significant (or contrastive) classes (or groups or bundles or units) called *phonemes*, which are in contrast with other phonemes in the same language. (The different phonemes of a language are analogically similar to the different countries of the U.N.) Phones are absolute and universal. Phonemes are relative to individual languages. Each language has its own groups of sounds or classes of sounds or phonemes.

Some sounds (phones) that a phonetician can hear and describe, even native speakers may not be aware of. Native speakers are trained to hear (i.e. perceive and interpret) the contrastive (or significant) sound features (the phonemes) in their own language. These phonemes they will distinguish easily. But native speakers of any language are not trained to hear the non-contrastive phonetic varieties (or phones) in their own language. They might begin to hear them if these phones are pointed out to them, but they will not distinguish them easily all by themselves.

By significant sound features is meant those features that produce meaningful differences when compared with other significant sound features in the same language. That is, if one sound exchanged for another similar sound in an utterance changes the meaning of the other utterance, then it is a separate and independent phoneme. If, on the other hand, a sound exchanged for another similar sound in an utterance does not change the meaning of the utterances, then it is *not* a separate and independent phoneme from the other similar sound, but a submember of the same phoneme. Submembers of the same phoneme are called *allophones*.

For example, [t], [tʰ], and [d] are similar sounds. They are similar because they are all alveolar (or dental) stops. The only difference between them is that [t] is voiceless and unaspirated, [tʰ] is voiceless and aspirated, and [d] is voiced. Now in the English utterance (and here we are interested in the pronunciation, not the spelling) *This is my toe* [ʃis iz mai tʰou], if [t] is used instead of [tʰ], the utterance will not change in meaning. (It would be rather unnatural for a native speaker of English, though, to use [t] in such an utterance.) On the other hand, if [d] is used instead of [t], the utterance will change in meaning, becoming *This is my dough* [ʃis iz mai dou]. This would lead to the conclusion that, in English, [t] and [tʰ] are submembers or allophones of the same phoneme /t/ and that [d] is a separate and independent phoneme /d/. Square brackets are used to indicate phonetic or allophonic transcription, while bars are used to indicate phonemic transcription. The symbol representing the phoneme is a matter of choice. Usually the simplest allophonic symbol or the allophonic symbol used most frequently in the language is chosen.

For another example, [p] and [b] are similar phonetic sounds. (This is absolutely and universally true.) Both are bilabial stops. The difference between them is that [p] is voiceless and [b] is voiced. Now in the Arabic utterance [hæːʃæ ħæpsun] "This is a prison", a voiceless [p] is heard before voiceless [s]. (In Arabic speech, a voiceless [p] occurs before voiceless consonants.) But nowhere in the Arabic language does the exchange of [p] for [b] produce any difference in meaning. (Native speakers of Arabic will naturally hear a [b] in the utterance.) This would lead to the conclusion that in *Arabic*, [p] and [b] are submembers or allophones of the same phoneme /b/. In English, [p] and [b] are separate and independent phonemes /p/ and /b/, because of the contrast in meaning between such words as pill:bill, pat:bat, and prick:brick.

A discussion of phonemes is a discussion of the significant sound features in one particular language at a time. It would help to remember *that a phoneme is a contrastive sound unit in a language*; it is contrastive because it distinguishes meanings when exchanged for other phonemes in the language; it is a unit because it includes within it a number of phones (or allophones or allophonic varieties or phonetic varieties) which are not contrastive (i.e. which are non-contrastive) with each other. The allophones of consonants are called *contoids*: and the allophones of vowels are called *vocoids*. (See Pike, 1967.)

3. The Eme

Look at these two words:
phone (which is any speech sound) and
phoneme (which is a contrastive sound unit in a language).
The difference between them is the *eme*, which stands for the element or the concept of *contrastiveness*. (See Pike, 1967.)

The *element of contrastiveness* is a very significant part of our experience. How two individuals or two concepts or two objects differ from each other influences our behavior in life in varying degrees. Even with similar objects or identical twins, one would look for some contrastive element to tell them apart or to express some preference of one over the other.

Now look at these two words:
phone (which is any speech sound) and
phonetic (which refers to any speech sound quality).
A *phonetic variety* would be a non-contrastive speech sound quality. The difference between them is *etic*, which stands for a *non-contrastive element*.

Now look at these two words:
phone (which is any speech sound) and
phonemic (which refers to a contrastive sound quality).
The difference between them is *emic*, which stands for a contrastive element.

Eme, therefore, is a noun that means the *element or concept of contrastiveness; etic* is an adjective that means *non-contrastive;* and *emic* is an adjective that means *contrastive.*

These concepts or meanings apply in practically all of our experiences. Let us consider, for example, a *semiotic* behavior that may be interpreted in different ways in two different cultural settings. (*Semiotics* is the study of facial expressions and body movements as means of communication.) The case here would be the closing of four fingers in two or three sequential movements with the hand at above shoulder level and with the palm of the hand facing downward.

The gesture would be interpreted in the American culture to mean a *wave of hello or good-bye.* In a Middle Eastern culture, it would mean *come here.*

Now if the same gesture is used with the palm of the hand facing upward, the meaning would be *come here* in both cultures.

To apply the words *etic* and *emic* to this cultural phenomenon, we can say that both gestures (with the palm of the hand facing upward and downward) would be *culturetically different* in both cultures, while they would be *culturemically the same* in a Middle Eastern culture and *culturemically different* in the American culture. Any photographically different gesture would be automatically different culturetically. For the two gestures to be culturemically different, there would have to be a contrastively different meaning or interpretation given to them. Applied to speech sounds, a phonetic difference would be non-contrastive, while a phonemic difference would be contrastive in a particular language. (For more details on the subject, see Pike, 1967.)

Chapter Six

The English Consonants

1. Introduction

The sounds of English are of two types: the *segmental features* and the *supra-segmental (or prosodic) features*. The *segmental features* include the *consonants* and the *vowels*.

The English consonants are twenty-four in number. The word *consonant* is *phonemic*. In other words, the consonants of English are contrastive with each other. Naturally, as expected, these consonants would have *phonetic varieties* or *allophones*. The *allophones* of consonants are called *contoids*. The word consonant here does not, of course, refer to the consonant letters which are found in the English alphabet, but rather to the consonants as they are interpreted orally. *Consonants*, therefore, refer to sounds, not letters.

2. The English Consonants in a Chart

The chart of English consonants below arranges the consonants according to the types and points of articulation. The chart is followed by an example on each consonant. When you look at the chart and study it, remember that the *points of articulation* are arranged in the same fashion as the *parts of the vocal apparatus*, with the front of the mouth on the left and the back of the mouth on the right. There is no specific order for the types of articulation, although the order used here is quite common.

Chart of the English Consonants

Point of Articulation

Type of Articulation		Bilabial	Labio-dental	Inter-dental	Alveolar	Retroflex	Alveo-palatal	Palatal	Velar	Glottal
Stops	vl. vd.	p b			t d				k g	
Affricates	vl. vd.						tʃ dʒ			
Fricatives	vl. vd.		f v	θ ð	s z		ʃ ʒ			h
Nasals	vd.	m			n			ɲ		
Lateral	vd.				l					
Vibrant	vd.				r					
Semi-vowels	vd.	w						j		

vl.means voiceless (vocal cords not vibrating)
vd. means voiced (vocal cords vibrating)

Examples:

1	/p/:	pen	13	/ʃ/: shoe
2	/b/:	book	14	/ʒ/: measure
3	/t/:	table	15	/tʃ/: child
4	/d/:	day	16	/dʒ/: judge
5	/k/:	look	17	/h/: hand
6	/g/:	go	18	/m/: mouth
7	/f/:	fat	19	/n/: nose
8	/v/:	voice	20	/ŋ/: sing
9	/θ/:	thin	21	/l/: land
10	/ð/:	though	22	/r/: run
11	/s/:	sit	23	/w/: wet
12	/z/:	zoos	24	/j/: yes

3. The English Consonants Described

Following is a list of the English consonant phonemes and their major allophones. The allophones are described phonetically, and their distribution is given with examples.

Feature mode

manifestation

Distribution mode

phoneme	allophones	description, distribution, and examples
/p/	[p]	Voiceless, unaspirated bilabial stop. It occurs in complementary distribution[1] with [pʰ], the latter appearing only before a vowel in the beginning of stressed syllables and released in word final positions. /sʌpər/ [sʌpər] "supper".
	[pʰ]	Voiceless aspirated bilabial stop. See [p] above. /paip/ [pʰaipʰ] "pipe".
/t/	[t]	Voiceless unaspirated alveolar stop. It occurs in complementary distribution with [tʰ], the latter appearing only before a vowel in the beginning of stressed syllables and released in word final positions. /betər/ [betər] "better".
	[tʰ]	Voiceless aspirated alveolar stop. See [t] above. /tɔt/ [tʰɔtʰ] "taught".
/k/	[k]	Voiceless unaspirated velar stop. It occurs in complementary distribution with [kʰ], the latter appearing only before a vowel in the beginning of stressed syllables and released in word final positions. /lukiŋ/ [lukiŋ] "looking".
	[kʰ]	Voiceless aspirated velar stop. See [k] above. /kuk/ [kʰukʰ] "cook"
/b/	[b]	Voiced bilabial stop. It occurs in all positions. /bai/ [bai] "by"; /əbaut/ [əbautʰ] "about"; /klʌb/ [klʌb] "club".
/d/	[d]	Voiced alveolar stop. It occurs in all positions. /did/ [did] "did"; /ædiŋ/ [ædiŋ] "adding".

[1]Complementary distribution means that where one element occurs the other never occurs. For example, the total distribution of the phoneme /p/ is the sum of the complementary distribution of its allophones, [p], and [pʰ].

Feature mode   *Manifestation mode*   *Distribution mode*

/g/	[g]	Voiced velar stop. It occurs in all positions. /gein/ [gein] "gain"; /begiŋ/ [begiŋ] "begging"; /beg/ [beg] "beg".
/tʃ/	[tʃ]	Voiceless affricate made up of a voiceless alveolar stop followed by a voiceless alveo-palatal fricative. It occurs in all positions. /tʃu:z/ [tʃu:z] "choose"; /mætʃ/ [mætʃ] "match". (/tʃ/ may be considered a cluster.)
/dʒ/	[dʒ]	Voiced affricate made up of a voiced alveolar stop followed by a voiced alveo-palatal fricative. It occurs in all positions. /dʒʌdʒ/ [dʒʌdʒ] "judge"; /eidʒiŋ/ [eidʒiŋ] "aging". (/dʒ/ may be considered a cluster.)
/f/	[f]	Voiceless labio-dental fricative. It occurs in all positions. /flai/ [flai] "fly"; /seifəst/ [seifəst] "safest; /if/ [if] "if".
/v/	[v]	Voiced labio-dental fricative. It occurs in all positions. /veil/ [veil] "veil"; /givən/ [givən] "given". /lʌv/ [lʌv] "love".
/θ/	[θ]	Voiceless inter-dental fricative. It occurs in all positions. /θiŋ/ [θiŋ] "thing"; /nʌθiŋ/ [nʌθiŋ] nothing"; /miθ/ [miθ] "myth".
/ð/	[ð]	Voiced inter-dental fricative. It occurs in all positions. /ðen/ [ðen] "then"; /wiðin/ [wiðin] "within"; /beið/ [beið] "bathe".
/s/	[s]	Voiceless alveolar fricative. It occurs in all positions. /sits/ [sits] "sits"; /lisən/ [lisən] "listen".
/z/	[z]	Voiced alveolar fricative. It occurs in all positions. /zu:z/ [zu:z] "zoos"; /bizi:/ [bizi:] "busy".
/ʃ/	[ʃ]	Voiceless alveo-palatal fricative. It occurs in all positions. /ʃu:/ [ʃu:] "shoe"; /wiʃiŋ/ [wiʃiŋ] "wishing"; /fiʃ/

[fiʃ] "fish".

/ʒ/   [ʒ]   Voiced alveo-palatal fricative. It occurs only in medial positions. /meʒər/ [meʒər] "measure".

/m/   [m]   Voiced bilabial nasal. It occurs in all positions. /mai/ [mai] "my"; /eimiŋ/ [eimiŋ] "aiming"; /neim/ [neim] "name".

/n/   [n]   Voiced alveolar nasal. It occurs in all positions. /nʌn/ [nʌn] "none"; /miːniŋ/ [miːniŋ] "meaning".

/ŋ/   [ŋ]   Voiced velar nasal. It occurs only in medial and final positions. /siŋiŋ/ [siŋiŋ] "singing".

/l/   [l]   Voiced alveolar lateral. It occurs in all positions. /liliː/ [liliː] "lily"; /bɔl/ [bɔl] "ball". In some English dialects, the [l] after a vowel is a little darker (or backed).

/r/   [r]   Voiced retroflex vibrant. It occurs in all possitions. /rɔr/ [rɔr] "roar"; /mæriː/ [mæriː] "marry". (In some English dialects, the [r] is a flapped alveolar vibrant, which is produced by having the tongue tip hit the alveolar ridge.)

/h/   [h]   Voiceless glottal fricative. It occurs only in initial and medial positions. /hænd/ [hænd] "hand"; /haushould/ [haushould] "household".

/w/   [w]   Voiced bilabial semi-vowel. It occurs in all positions. /wel/ [wel] "well"; /louər/ [louər] "lower"; /lou/ [lou] or /low/ [low] "low".

/j/   [j]   Voiced palatal semi-vowel. It occurs in all positions. /jes/ [jes] "yes"; /flaiiŋ/ [flaiiŋ] or /flajiŋ/ [flajiŋ] "flying"; /flai/ [flai] or /flaj/ [flaj] "fly".

4. The English Consonant Clusters

A consonant cluster is a combination of two or more consonants. Such clusters may occur in initial, medial, or final positions. A few examples are given here.

a. Initial clusters with two consonants:

/pr/ "pray"	/bj/ "beautiful"	/st/ "stay"
/pl/ "play"	/dr/ "dry"	/sp/ "speak"
/pj/ "pure"	/dw/ "dwarf"	/sm/ "smell"
/tr/ "tray"	/gr/ "grand"	/sk/ "skim"
/tw/ "twig"	/gl/ "glow"	/sl/ "sleep"
/kr/ "crane"	/fr/ "frame"	/sf/ "sphere"
/kl/ "clam"	/fl/ "fly"	/sn/ "snap"
/kw/ "quiet"	/fj/ "fume"	/sw/ "swim"
/kj/ "curious"	/vj/ "view"	/ʃr/ "shred"
/br/ "bray"	/mj/ "muting"	/hj/ "hew"
/bl/ "blow"	/θr/ "throw"	

b. Initial clusters with three consonants:

/spl/ "spleen"	/skw/ "squat"	/skr/ "scream"
/skj/ "skewer"	/spr/ "spray"	

c. Medial clusters with two consonants:

/ks/ "accept"	/ts/ "itself"	/rm/ "army"
/kj/ "acute"	/tʃ/ "catching"	/rɖ/ "worthy"
/kr/ "accrue"	/ft/ "lifting"	/rn/ "warning"
/pt/ "accepted"	/nt/ "wanted"	/sr/ "crossroad"
/pr/ "approve"	/nʃ/ "mention"	/st/ "casting"
/ks/ "mixing"	/rk/ "working"	/sk/ "asking"
/rk/ "market"	/rt/ "carting"	/ʃr/ "mushroom"

d. Medial clusters with three consonants:

/mpl/ "complete"	/str/ "administration
/mpt/ "empty"	/kst/ "sixteen"
/nst/ "constant"	/nsp/ "inspire"
/ksp/ "expect"	/ntr/ "intrigue"

e. Medial clusters with four consonants:

/nstr/ "construct"	/rldl/ "wordly"
/kstr/ "extra"	/kskl/ "exclude"

f. Final clusters with two consonants:

/ps/ "cups"	/rf/ "dwarf"	/nz/ "tins"
/pt/ "kept"	/rʃ/ "marsh"	/lθ/ "wealth"
/ts/ "cats"	/rz/ "bars"	/ld/ "hold"
/tθ/ "eighth"	/θs/ "baths"	/lz/ "balls"
/ks/ "kicks"	/ʃd/ "soothed"	/lk/ "silk"
/kt/ "looked"	/dθ/ "breadth"	/rk/ "hark"
/bd/ "rubbed"	/dz/ "lads"	/rt/ "dirt"
/bz/ "rubs"	/gd/ "begged"	/rθ/ "worth"
/ŋd/ "banged"	/gz/ "dogs"	/rd/ "bird"
/ŋk/ "thank"	/ft/ "gift"	/rz/ "cars"
/ŋθ/ "length"	/fθ/ "fifth"	/rm/ "firm"
/ŋz/ "wings"	/fs/ "cuffs"	/rb/ "curb"
/lt/ "melt"	/vd/ "loved"	/rl/ "curl"
/ls/ "false"	/vz/ "loves"	/rv/ "nerve"
/lz/ "walls"	/md/ "summed"	/ʒz/ "soothes"
/lf/ "myself"	/mp/ "ramp"	/sp/ "lisp"
/lp/ "help"	/mz/ "rams"	/st/ "must"
/rn/ "darn"	/nt/ "bent"	/sk/ "risk"
/rl/ "curl"	/ns/ "mince"	/zd/ "phased"
/rp/ "sharp"	/nd/ "mend"	/ʃt/ "finished"

g. Final clusters with three consonants:

/pts/ "corrupts"	/fθs/ "fifths"	/rnd/ "burned"
/tθs/ "eighths"	/mps/ "ramps"	/rmd/ "farmed"
/kts/ "pacts"	/mpt/ "cramped"	/rlz/ "curls"
/kst/ "fixed"	/ndz/ "mends"	/rmz/ "firms"
/ksθ/ "sixth"	/lmz/ "helms"	/nθs/ "months"
/lks/ "sulks"	/rks/ "harks"	/lts/ "faults"
/lkt/ "sulked"	/rkt/ "harked"	/rld/ "curled"
/ldz/ "molds"	/rst/ "burst"	/rnz/ "burns"
/dθs/ "breadths"	/rts/ "carts"	/rvz/ "curves"
/fts/ "lifts"	/rdz/ "birds"	/sks/ "masks"
/ŋkt/ "instinct"		

h. Final clusters with four consonants:

/ksts/ "contexts"	/rsts/ "bursts"
/ksθs/ "sixths"	/rldz/ "worlds"
/mpts/ "attempts"	/ŋkts/ "instincts"

5.   Length in English Consonants

Length means the time it takes to produce sounds. This does *not* mean the speed at which a person speaks. It means, rather, the *relative* length of time in which each separate sound is produced, as compared with a longer or shorter time in which the same sound or other sounds may be produced in the stream of speech. If the variation in the relative length of sounds in any language produces a variation in the meaning of an utterance, then length is a significant sound feature in that language;   that is, it is phonemic. But if the variation in the relative length of sounds produces no variation in meaning, then length is a non-significant or non-contrastive sound feature in that language; that is; it is phonetic and non-phonemic.

Length in most English dialects is not phonemic. This does not mean, however, that there is no phonetic length in consonants and vowels.   On the contrary, variations in the length of segmental phonemes appear regularly, depending on the surrounding sounds. But this change in length does not result in any change in meaning. The only place where length in consonants is meaningful is when one word ends with the same consonant as the following word begins. For example; *red dress, put together, come my way, far right*, etc.

Chapter Seven

The English Vowels

1. Introduction

There is considerable uniformity in the consonant sounds of English across the many dialectical varieties of Standard English. Unlike the consonants, however, the vowel sounds present more varieties and more potential problems for ESL/EFL learners.

In Standard American English, there may be a general acceptance of 13 vowel sounds and three diphthongs, making a total of 16 vowel sounds as compared with five vowel letters in the alphabet. A *diphthong* is a significant (contrastive) glide from one quality vowel to another.

In Standard British English, there are five additional vowel sounds: one single vowel and four diphthongs. Besides, the distribution of some of the vowels in certain words is not always the same in both American and British English, giving rise occasionally to some confusion. For example, while the *a* in *hat* is pronounced /æ/ in both, and the *a* in *father* is pronounced /a/ in both, British English would normally have /a/ and American English /æ/ in such words as *class, glass, France, pass, ask, mask, can't, shan't*, etc. The first vowel sound in *neither* and *either* would be /ai/ in British English and /i:/ in American English. In some words, one would likely witness different vowel qualities, different silent vowels, and different stresses in both American and British English. A good example would be *laboratory* (pronounced /lǽbrətɔ̀ri:/ in American English and /ləbɔ́rətri:/ in

British English). Similar varieties occur in such words as *customary, ordinary, derogatory,* etc. /ɔ/ in American English is usually pronounced a little further forward, making it closer to /a/ as in *ball, fall, caught, law,* etc. The /ou/ in American English in such words as *oh, no, note, coat,* etc. is pronounced with a bigger glide in British English, making it go from /ə/ to /u/, hence /əu/, /nəu/, /nəut/, and /kəut/, respectively.

2. The English Vowels in a Chart

The chart of the English vowels below arranges the vowels according to their point of articulation in the mouth. It would be helpful to remember that in this chart, as in the chart of the consonants, the left side represents the front of the mouth and the right side the back of the mouth. It is also important to know the meanings of the words used in this chart.

a. *Front, central, back, high, mid,* and *low* refer to the position of the tongue in the mouth.

b. *Rounded* and *unrounded* refer to the shape of the lips.

c. *Close* and *open* refer to the relative opening of the jaw.

Chart of the English Vowels

		FRONT Unrounded	FRONT Rounded	CENTRAL Unrounded	CENTRAL Rounded	BACK Unrounded	BACK Rounded
HIGH	Close	iː					uː
HIGH	Open	i					u
MID	Close	ei		ə əː			ou
MID	Open	e		ʌ			ɒ
LOW	Close	æ					ɔ
LOW	Open			a			

Examples:

1 /i:/:	seat	8 /ə:/:	bird (always followed by /r/)
2 /i/:	sit	9 /a/:	f*a*ther
3 /ei/:	main	10 /u:/:	pool
4 /e/:	men	11 /u/:	pull
5 /æ/:	cat	12 /ou/:	note
6 /ə/:	*a*bove	13 /ɒ/:	hot (not found in American
	(unstressed)		English)
7 /ʌ/:	ab*o*ve	14 /ɔ/:	ball
	(stressed)		

Vowel number 13 (/ɒ/) is used in British English in such words as *hot, dot, spot, contrast*, etc.

In some dialects of American English, vowel number 1 (/i:/) is sometimes pronounced with an audible glide as though it were /ij/. Also vowel number 10 (/u:/) is sometimes pronounced with an equally audible glide as though it were /uw/. *Peel* and *pool* would be examples of the above vowels respectively.

Most speakers of American English would pronounce vowel numbers 3 and 12 (/ei/ and /ou/) with very audible glides as in *laid* and *load* respectively. This is not the case in other dialects of English (e.g. Scottish) where the first element in both vowels is made slightly longer.

The diphthongs are three in number:

/ai/: high
/au/: how
/ɔi/: boy

Other diphthongs that exist in British English but not in American English are:

/iə/: here
/eə/: there
/uə/: poor
/ɔə/: door

3. The English Vowels Described

Following is a list of the English vowel phonemes. They are described phonetically, and their distribution is given with examples.

(handwritten) late   ei   e closed
let   e   ɛ   open

phoneme	allophones	description, distribution, and examples
/i:/	[i:]	High close front unrounded. It occurs in all positions. /i:t/ [i:t] "eat"; /pli:z/ [pli:z] "please"; /bi:/ [bi:] "bee".
/i/	[i]	High open front unrounded. It occurs only initially and medially. /in/ [in] "in"; /liv/ [liv] "live".
/ei/	[ei]	Mid close front unrounded. It occurs in all positions. /eim/ [eim] "aim"; /neim/ [neim] "name"; /dei/ [dei] "day".
/e/	[e]	Mid open front unrounded. It occurs only initially and medially. /end/ [end] "end"; /send/ [send] "send".
/æ/	[æ]	Low close front unrounded. It occurs only initially and medially. /æd/ [æd] "add"; /sæŋ/ [sæŋ] "sang".
/ə/	[ə]	Mid close central unrounded. It is unstressed and occurs in all positions. /əbaut/ [əbaut] "about"; /sentrəl/ [sentrəl] "central"; /aidiə/ [aidiə] "idea".
/ə:/	[ə:]	Mid close central unrounded. It is always followed by [r], although in some dialects the [r] is not pronounced. It occurs only initially and medially. /ə:rθ/ [ə:rθ] "earth"; /bə:rd/ [bə:rd] "bird".
/ʌ/	[ʌ]	Mid open central unrounded. It is stressed and occurs only initially and medially. /ʌp/ [ʌp] "up"; /sʌn/ [sʌn] "sun".
/a/	[a]	Low open central unrounded. It

		occurs in all positions. /art/ [art] "art"; /smart/ [smart] "smart"; /ma/ [ma] "ma (mother)".
/u:/	[u:]	High close back rounded. It occurs in all positions. /u:z/ [u:z] "ooze"; /smu:ʃ/ [smu:ʃ] "smooth"; /zu:/ [zu:] "zoo".
/u/	[u]	High open back rounded. It occurs only medially. /wud/ [wud] "wood".
/ou/	[ou]	Mid close back rounded. It occurs in all positions. /oun/ [oun] "own"; /stoun/ [stoun] "stone"; /nou/ [nou] "no".
/ɒ/	[ɒ]	Mid open back rounded. It occurs only initially and medially. /ɒn/ [ɒn] "on"; /bɒnd/ [bɒnd] "bond". (This sound does not exist in American English, where [a] is usually used instead.)
/ɔ/	[ɔ]	Low close back rounded. It occurs in all positions. /ɔl/ [ɔl] "all"; /bɔl/ [bɔl] "ball"; /lɔ/ [lɔ] "law".

4. Length in English Vowels

Length in English vowels is also not phonemic, although variations in vowel length exist. In English, the phonemes /i: ei u: ou ə: a/ are phonetically longer that the other vowels. In addition, each vowel may vary in its phonetic length, depending on the sounds following it. The following examples of different phonetic lengths for the phoneme /i:/ are given (in order of length):

   (a) b*ee* (in final position) - longest
   (b) b*ee*s (before a voiced fricative)
   (c) b*ea*m (before a nasal)
   (d) s*ee*d (before a voiced stop)
   (e) p*ie*ce (before a voiceless fricative)
   (f) b*ea*t (before a voiceless stop) - shortest

Diphthongs are long because of the time it takes to produce both elements.

Chapter Eight

The English Prosodic Features

1. Introduction

The English prosodic features - or the English supra-segmental features - are five in number: stress, intonation, pause, juncture, and rhythm. All these are part of the phonological system of English. Speakers use them to elicit meanings, and listeners hear them and respond to them. These features have traditionally not been given much importance in learning-teaching situations probably because they are not adequately (and sometimes not at all) represented on the written or printed page.

For an analogy, if you have ever seen a mason build a brick wall, you will probably have noticed that the bricks are placed side by side and stacked up on top of each other. These bricks resemble the segmental features of sound; the bricks are the individual segments that make up the wall. But no wall can stand for long or be worth much if there is no cement (or some cementing element) to hold the bricks together. While each brick has a distinct beginning and a distinct end, the cement does not appear that way. It would be awfully difficult to say with any degree of precision what specific part of the cement belongs to each brick. The cement is a super or supra element that goes over a number of bricks at a time.

The prosodic features of a language are like the cement in our analogy; they are the super or supra elements (the supra-segmental features) that are used over more than one segment (or sound) at a time.   They are so important in speech that if they are produced correctly, listeners would more readily understand speakers even if the speakers make a few errors in the production of certain consonants and vowels.

The description and functions of the five prosodic features of English are presented in brief and simple terms, with examples, only to point out to teachers that the role played by prosodic features is of extreme importance in understanding and producing speech.

2. Stress
Stress is the force of breath with which sounds are produced.   This force is relative; that is, the strength or weakness of the force is determined in relation to other forces of breath in the utterance or utterances of a person.   For example, in the word *market*, it is clear that the first syllable has a stronger stress than the second syllable.

Stress in English is not fixed.   There is no way of knowing in advance where the different stress levels will occur in English speech. Not all linguists agree as to the number of relative stress phonemes in English.   Some believe that there are four phonemic word stress levels:

(in order of loudness)
       (a) primary stress - symbol: / '/
       (b) secondary stress - symbol: /ᵛ/
       (c) tertiary stress - symbol: / ` /
       (d) weak stress - symbol: / / (no mark)
For example: élevàtor ŏperàtor or ĕlevàtor óperàtor

Other linguists believe that there are only three phonemic word stress levels in English with the addition of a sentence stress that moves according to the meaning of the utterance:

(in order of loudness)
       (a) primary stress - symbol: / ' /
       (b) secondary stress - symbol: / ` /
       (c) weak stress - symbol: / / (no mark)

For example: yés, márket, administrátion.
Examples of sentence stress:
The *boy* saw the dog. (boy, not girl)
The boy *saw* the dog. (saw, not called)
The boy saw the *dog.* (dog, not cat)
The greater the number of contrastive elements in a language, the more difficult it is to teach it and to learn it, especially as a second or foreign language. The three-stress theory for English is, from a teaching point of view, more practical, particularly because of the fact that native speakers of English do not easily distinguish four different stress levels (phonemes). Also, for practical teaching purposes, it is important to give more attention to the primary stress level because of the meaning contrasts it yields.

3. Intonation
Intonation means the changes in the pitch (or music) of the voice while producing speech. Every utterance is produced with some intonation and pitch. Pitch levels, like stress levels, are relative to each other. In tone languages, pitch is fixed: it is absolute. In other languages, intonational pitch levels are relative: they change from person to person.

It is not the pitches by themselves that produce meanings beyond the meanings of the words and grammatical structures of an utterance; rather, it is the combination of different pitches or levels of intonation and their formation as *glides* or *contours* that does that. In an English sentence, there will usually be two pitch parts:

(a) the pre-contour, which occurs before a stressed syllable, and
(b) the primary contour, which begins with the stressed syllable. (See examples below.)

In English, there are four phonemic pitch levels. These are given numbers and names:

4 _____	high
3 _____	high - mid
2 _____	low - mid
1 _____	low

Examples: (The small zero sign indicates primary stress.)

(a) <u>The boy went to the °3⌐ mar ⌐ ket</u>
    2-   1 ⌐___

or <u>The boy went to the market</u>
   2-   °3 -1

(b) (Counting) <u>One, two, three, four, five.</u>
                  °2-3 °2-3   °2-3 °2-3 °3-1

(c) <u>Oh, John.</u>
   °4-1 °4-1

(d) <u>He came.</u>
   2- °3-1

  <u>Who? The boy?</u>
 °2-3   2   °2-3

  <u>Yes.</u>
 °3-1

(e) <u>When I went home, I found the book.</u>
    2-   °3-2   2-   °3-1

(f) <u>I bought books, ink, pencils, and paper.</u>
   2-   °3-2 °3-2 °3- 2   2   °3-1

(g) <u>I saw John.</u>
   2   °3-1

  <u>Who?</u>
  °2-3

  <u>John</u>
 °3-1

(h) <u>I saw someone.</u>
   2-   °3-1

  <u>Who?</u>
 °3-1

  <u>John</u>
 °3-1

(i) <u>Is John home?</u>
   2-   °3-1

  <u>No.</u>
 °3-1

or <u>Is John at home?</u>
    2-   °2-3

  <u>No</u>
 °3-1

4. Pause

Pause is the length of silence between parts of an utterance. In English, there are two pause phonemes. (Some linguists believe that there are three pause phonemes.) The two pause phonemes are a *short* one and a *final* one. The symbols used for these phonemes are a single bar for the short pause and a double bar for the final pause.

For example: Go/he said//

This/however/is good//

Understanding these pause phonemes and knowing how to use them is part of learning and teaching English.

5. Juncture

Juncture is really a very short pause; it is the space in speech between sounds or words. In English, there is one juncture phoneme. The symbol for this juncture phoneme is /+/ (a plus sign). In the examples that follow, one can see how this *plus juncture* operates in contrast with the absence of the juncture or in contrast with a different position for it:

(a) I scream   /ái+skrí:m/
    ice cream   /àis+krí:m/

(b) a name   /ə+néim/
    an aim   /ənéim/

Putting this juncture in the wrong place may change the meaning of an utterance or even turn it into an utterance that might not be understood.

6. Rhythm

Rhythm means the beat of language. In English, rhythm is stress-timed. This means that the time between two primary stresses is the same. If there are many words or syllables between the two primary stresses, then these syllables will be pronounced fast: this is why native speakers of English jam their syllables. If, on the other hand, there is only a small number of syllables between the primary stresses, then these syllables will be pronounced slowly and more clearly. For example:

(a) Can you sée the dóctor?

(b) Can you sée the tall dóctor?

(c) Can you sée the tall and handsome dóctor?

Here the words *see* and *doctor* take primary stresses for special purposes. Now in (a) there is only one word between them: in (b) there are two words; and in (c) there are four words. All the words between *see* and *doctor* will take the same time to produce. This is the reason why the words in the second sentence will be produced faster than in the first; and in the third sentence, the words will be produced the fastest.

In learning to understand native English speech, it is necessary to understand jammed syllables and words.

7. Conclusion

The presentation of English prosodic features has been brief. For practical purposes, though, the information here has two major objectives:

a. It is sufficient to make teachers realize that the supra-segmental elements of English (as in any other language) are a very significant and integral part of the phonological system.

b. It implies that some serious attention needs to be given to the supra-segmental features in the teaching of English phonology so that ESL/EFL learners can understand the stream of speech in English and produce it well enough to be understood.

Chapter Nine

Language Acquisition

1. First Language Acquisition

"Look at my foots! They're wet," said the three-year-old nursery school girl. No teacher, or parent, should be disturbed by the youngster's use of *foots*. It is very natural and should be expected if the child has learned *mat/mats*, *bat/bats*, and *foot*, but has not come across the item *feet*.

All human beings have been endowed with certain faculties (powers or abilities) that make it possible for them to learn language. Animal language (or system of communication) is instinctive. A French dog raised in Japan will respond to dog calls in America in the same way as any other American dog. The length of time of a bee dance will be given the same distance-to-flower interpretation by all local and foreign bees. All elephants (related or unrelated, local or foreign) within a one mile radius will raise their ears at the very same time or make a simultaneous move in the very same direction upon sensing some low frequency infra-sound produced by one of their kind in the area.

Human beings are different. Our language is acquired, and we acquire it by the use of the faculties we are endowed with. We are endowed with the ability to hear with discrimination. This needs to be explained. Hearing is not the same as listening. Listening (with understanding) is one of the four language skills. (The others are speaking, reading, and writing.) But one can listen and not hear. What is it that we hear in our native language? We hear the distinctive (or contrastive) sound features, and we do not naturally hear the non-contrastive sound features in our own native language. For example, we hear the difference (we discriminate) between the sound /p/ and the sound /b/ in such words as *pill/bill* and *staple/stable* . But no native speaker of English would naturally (ie, without tutoring in phonetics) hear the phonetic difference between the two non-contrastive [p] sounds in *pill* and *staple.* In the first instance, it is an aspirated [pʰ] sound; in the second, it is an unaspirated [p] sound. But speakers of Chinese would hear them because in their language these two sounds are contrastive - ie, the difference between them produces a difference in meaning just as the /p/ and /b/ sounds produce the difference between *pill* and *bill* in English.

By the age of two or two and a half, children normally have established the basic phonological structures or system of their first or native language. This system is essentially a neuro-psychophysiological system. Children, by that age, have developed the ability to *hear* the distinctive (contrastive, phonemic) sounds of their language and discriminate between them. They can recognize different meanings of utterances (single words or longer linguistic constructions) when these meanings are signaled only by a difference of two contrastive sounds. (By that age they can also approximate the production of these contrastive sounds and discriminate between them.) The same principle applies to the recognition of the grammatical system of the language by children. By *grammatical system* is meant the patterns of word forms (morphology) and word order (syntax). This is the fundamental basis of children's language acquisition.

We are also endowed with the ability to speak (utter, produce) language with discrimination. Children who have acquired the proper hearing habits of the phonological system will be able to produce that same system (unless there is some speech impediment) and make judgements about it. They can hear themselves make a mistake and correct it (occasionally with a smile). And children who have learned (as part of the grammatical system) such items as *mat/mats, rat/rats, bit/bits, ship/ships,* and *cap/caps* will, upon learning the unitary items *foot* and *sheep* , produce (without hesitation) the plural counterparts *foots* and *sheeps* and judge them as correct until they are taught that the language system, in actual use and practice, is not as perfect as their own innate analysis has shown.

When my daughter was two and a half years old, she heard me tell my son (who is less than a year older) that he could go in the car with me if he ate his lunch. Not wanting her brother to enjoy the ride without earning it by fulfilling the condition, she turned to me and said, "If he *doos* he'll go and if he *don'ts* he *won'ts*." I picked her up and kissed her saying, "You're a born linguist!"

We are endowed with the ability to substitute and expand with discrimination. Because of the built-in language competence we have, we are able to produce an unlimited number of utterances and to judge them as correct. For example, here is a sentence that I am sure no person has come across in this form before: "Once there happened to be a king of a prosperous country whose sister was made, after years of struggle, intrigue and cunning, queen of the not-so-prosperous neighboring country." Anyone who has a command of Modern Standard English will judge this sentence to be correct if heard, spoken or written. At a very early age (between two and three), children begin to demonstrate this ability to substitute and expand with discrimination. This ability grows and develops, depending upon interest, use of language and exposure to various forms of language through conversation, reading, writing, and the media.

Two simple, but significant, cautions must be made. Do not repeat baby talk or child language yourself as a means of communicating more intimately with your children. Their greatest need is for a consistent model. Stick to your own best language form. Also, do not be too anxious to correct your children's language bluntly. If an incorrect, but more natural, form is uttered, you might want to utter the correct form yourself, but do it by the way and let it pass.

One of the most fascinating aspects of child rearing is the observation of language use and development. Exposing children to good forms of language at home through selected books and T.V. programs is of immense value.

2. Second Language Acquisition

On the basis of the three major endowments discussed above and with the experience gained in learning our first (usually native) language, we are very capable of acquiring one or more other languages. With youngsters this ability to learn other languages is at its best and strongest, primarily because inhibitions are at their lowest (practically nonexistent) and because their capacity to absorb language (receptive ability) and to repeat or mimic it (productive ability) is at a very high level. Parents with bilingual or trilingual children at the ages of four and five can attest to this great advantage. There should be no hesitation to expose children to a second language at the age of two or three and to even a third language at the age of four or five, especially if the exposure is to native speakers of these languages.

The elements or component parts of language (pronunciation, vocabulary, and grammar, which are often referred to as phonology, morphology, and syntax) must be learned on two levels: the *receptive level* and the *productive level*. In other words, learning the elements of language means both understanding them and using them. The degree of learners' receptive ability in language is measured by the speed and correctness with which they understand what they hear or read. And the degree of their productive ability in language is measured by the speed and correctness with which they speak or write.

Of the three language elements, it is vocabulary that is learned with the greatest conscious and cognitive effort. The other two elements (pronunciation and grammar) are learned more *habitually* (especially in the case of pronunciation). This is particularly important in the development of proficiency in *language usage*, which entails a command of the *forms* of language. The conscious or cognitive effort applies more to *language use,* which entails a command of the *choice of the right forms to be applied in appropriate situations.*

The development of both of these competencies (in language *usage* and language *use*) can only be reached through practice. Especially is this true in the development of proficiency in pronunciation where habits are formed.

The habits formed in learning our first language are very strong. They are so strong that learners of a second language carry the first language habits across language boundaries, thereby coloring second language production with first language features. This is particularly true of pronunciation and grammar. If you know something about Arabic, Greek, French, German, and Spanish pronunciation, for example, you will readily recognize the speakers of these languages when they use English, because they color their English production with Arabic, Greek, French, German, and Spanish features.

In learning a second or foreign language, therefore, learners have one strong factor in their favor and one strong factor introducing hurdles. The factor in their favor is the fact that they have already learned a (first) language, which has given them the experience of handling language as a system and a means of communication. The factor presenting hurdles is the set of habits they have developed in the phonological and grammatical systems of their first language. This means that there are two major types of new habits to be learned in the second or foreign language: habits which are entirely new to them and habits which need to replace old habits. Of these two types of habits to be acquired, the latter is usually more difficult because it involves some process of unlearning.

More will be said about second or foreign language acquisition in later chapters dealing with learning and teaching methods.

3. English as a Second or Foreign Language

English has become virtually a world language. It is the most widely taught and learned second or foreign language in the world. Teachers of English as a second or foreign language are in demand everywhere: in English speaking countries as well as abroad. Around the globe, of course, the vast majority of teachers of English are non-native speakers of English, which means that the majority of learners of English are exposed to a good number of English varieties that are colored to varying degrees (especially phonologically) by other languages.

Why is there such a global rush to learn English? The widespread use of English is, of course, the main reason. More specifically, English is the main language of communication in the world. About one half of the world's newspapers and telephone communications are in English; more than one half of the world's faxes, telexes, and telegraphs are in English; much more than half the computer data in the world is in English; communication between airline pilots and ground controls is predominantly in English around the world; the main language of trade, business, banking, science, technology, and movies is in English; and English is spoken by about one eighth of the world's population as a first or native language. One should not wonder, then, that about half the world's population learns English as a second or foreign language.

The difference between English as a second language and English as a foreign language is a distinction in how English is to be used by the learner. If English is to be used outside the classroom as a medium of communication in everyday life, then it is a second language, especially for speakers of other languages who end up living in English speaking countries such as Australia, Canada, Great Britain, New Zealand, and the U.S.A. If, on the other hand, English is to be used in the language class and sporadically (or even for specific purposes) outside the classroom, then it is learned as a foreign language.

It is equally desirable for speakers of English (especially in the U.S.A) to learn a foreign language.   There are, of course, academic and business motives for doing that: research, translation, correspondence, understanding invoices, and so on.   But there are also life pleasures involved: reading a headline or a sign in a foreign country; saying Hello! or How are you? to an international visitor; and, in a more sophisticated way, reading a foreign newspaper, magazine, story or novel; corresponding with a pen-pal across the seas; learning about different cultures; widening one's own intellectual and cultural horizons; enriching one's life and basking in the abundance.

Unfortunately, however, many foreign language classes are simply not interesting, not exciting, not relevant, not functional, not communicative, and not natural.   There is that insistence on sticking to that boring textbook, on looking up a list of words, on writing so many sentences, on doing that unnecessary grammar exercise.   No wonder students hate the experience.   On the other hand, we know of cases that have been dynamic and motivating.   Much depends upon the teacher, the syllabus and the materials and activities in a school or program. Making a foreign language relevant or more relevant to students' lives is the key to motivation and effectiveness.

Chapter Ten

Types of Contrastive Analysis in Applied Linguistics

1. Introduction

Modern linguistic science has contributed very much towards making the teaching and learning of foreign languages more successful. The greatest help from linguistic science has come from the area of contrastive linguistics. Here the various types of contrastive analysis are presented briefly.

2. A Contrastive Phonological Analysis

A contrastive phonological analysis is, of course, based on a phonemic analysis of two languages: the learners' native language and the target language (the language to be learned). Such a phonemic analysis will give the linguist the phonological structures of both languages. These structures will include the segmental and the supra-segmental elements in both languages. It would actually determine:

(a) the phonemes of each language,
(b) the allophones (or phonetic variations) of these phonemes, and
(c) the distribution of the allophones.

The contrastive phonological analysis would reveal the theoretical phonemic and phonetic and distributional problems that a learner would face in learning a target (second or foreign) language. Such a contrastive analysis would determine:

(a) whether a phoneme in the target language exists in the learner's native language,

(b) (if the phoneme exists) whether the allophones are phonetically the same or different in number and quality, and

(c) whether the allophones have the same or different distributional patterns in both languages.

3. A Contrastive Morphemic Analysis

A contrastive morphemic analysis is based on a morphemic analysis of both languages. The morphemic analysis would determine:

(a) what the morphemic forms are in each language,

(b) whether the meanings of the morphemes are similar or different, and

(c) whether the morphemes are combined and distributed in similar or different ways in both languages.

4. A Contrastive Syntactic Analysis

A contrastive syntactic analysis is based on a syntactic analysis of both languages. The syntactic analysis would determine:

(a) what the word order is in each language,

(b) what meanings are given by different word order arrangements, and

(c) how different words are combined and distributed.

The contrastive syntactic analysis would determine:

(a) how the order of words differs in both languages,

(b) what meanings are given by different word order arrangements, and

(c) whether the combination of words is distributed in similar or different ways in both languages.

5. A Contrastive Lexical Analysis

A contrastive lexical analysis would determine, at each learning level, what words are used and what their coverage of meaning is. Different meanings for each word are a natural feature of all languages. No two languages, however, have their words cover the same area of meaning. Many language problems are caused by translation, assuming, wrongly of course, that a word in one language covers the same area of meaning as in another language.

6. A Contrastive Contextual and Cultural Analysis

A contrastive contextual and cultural analysis is, of course, not linguistic in nature, but it is related to linguistics and language learning. The same words or sentences in two different contexts or cultures might have very different meanings. A contrastive contextual and cultural analysis helps teachers and learners of foreign languages understand the target language better, and it also helps them produce the right utterances in the right contexts and cultural situations.

7. A Contrastive Semiotic Analysis

In order to communicate well and successfully in a second or foreign language and in a foreign cultural situation, it is important for teachers and learners to know what devices (other than sound) are used to communicate ideas and meanings. Some of these devices may be facial expressions, gestures, and other bodily movements. Even if the right words are used, if they are accompanied by the wrong gesture or facial expression, a different (or wrong) message may be communicated.

8. An Error Analysis

An error analysis determines the actual problems that learners face in learning the target language. While other comparative linguistic analyses tell us in advance what theoretical problems learners will face, an error analysis tells us really what mistakes they actually do make. This type of analysis is of great help to classroom teachers; it tells them what new or additional materials and methods they need to use to solve real problems of learners.

9. An Analysis of Constructive and Destructive Interference

An analysis of the constructive and destructive interference from one language to another goes beyond contrastive analysis and error analysis. In a contrastive analysis, we arrive at the theoretical linguistic problems before teaching. In an error analysis, we discover what problems the learners are really facing and what mistakes they are actually making. In an analysis of constructive and destructive interference, we have an added aid to the teacher. An element which, in theory, is a problem according to the contrastive analysis may not prove to be a destructive element, but rather a constructive element in the process of teaching and learning.

For example, let us assume that a native speaker of English wants to learn Arabic (as a target language or foreign language). Among the phonological problems that this learner will face is the phonemic contrast between two [s] sounds: one is/s/ [s] (a voiceless alveolar fricative) and the other is /S/ [S] (a voiceless velarized fricative, as in /si:n/ [si:n] "the letter s" and /Si:n/ [Si:n] "China". The learner (a native speaker of English) distinguishes one phonemic /s/ in English, although there are several phonetic varieties of /s/ in English. In theory and in practice (according to both the contrastive analysis and the error analysis), the contrast between /s/ and /S/ in Arabic would be a problem.

The interference of the native language of the learner-in this case English-can be used constructively in teaching her/him to hear and produce these two sounds in Arabic. Varieties in the /s/ sound in English can be pointed out. For example, the /s/ in *sit* in English is very much like (probably the same as) the /s/ in /si:n/ in Arabic; but the /s/ in *salt* in English is closer to the /S/ in /Si:n/. Pointing this out to the learner can be the first constructive step towards making her/him hear and produce the two phonemic contrasts in Arabic.

An analysis of constructive and destructive interference can be shown on a scale with degrees going from a)very constructive interference to b)constructive interference to c)an area of no interference to d)destructive interference and finally to e)very destructive interference.

A constrastive phonological analysis, an error analysis, and an analysis of the constructive and destructive interference would be very helpful in teaching learners of English as a second or foreign language to hear and produce the sounds of English in the proper linguistic and social contexts.

Chapter Eleven

Sample Problems Facing ESL/EFL Learners

1. Introduction

This chapter is not meant to give the ESL/EFL teacher a complete list of the phonological problems facing ESL/EFL learners. It is, however, meant to indicate that when it comes to pronunciation (as well as to a great part of grammar), students of different language backgrounds will necessarily face very different problems learning English.

Because the development of pronunciation habits is so strong, learners of a second or foreign language tend to carry these habits across language boundaries. To the extent that these habits are different in different languages, they will manifest themselves as in need of different drills to ensure the mastery of English sounds.

2. Native Language Interference

We have all acquired a set of eating habits. What happens when we desire to change the pattern or patterns we are used to? We find that features of the old habits remain with us until we have had enough practice in the use of the new pattern or patterns.

The same is true of language. We have all acquired a set of linguistic habits by learning our native languages. Now, desiring to learn a second or foreign language, we find that features of the old habits remain with us, coloring the features of the new language system.

This is particularly true in the area of pronunciation; and it is for this very reason that native speakers of Arabic, Armenian, French, German, Italian, Portuguese, and Spanish, for example, speak English with an Arabic, French, German, Italian, Portuguese, or Spanish "accent".

Second or foreign language learning is an adjustment. It is an adjustment on the part of the learner to a new system. Like adjusting to a new set of dining-table habits or a new set of social habits, second or foreign language learning means adjusting to a new set of language habits.

The word *system* is used in reference to language because the nature of language (at least from a *usage* point of view) is such that it operates as a system of human behavior. The word *habit* is used in reference to second or foreign language learning because the signaling devices of the second or foreign language (especially phonology, morphology, and syntax again at least form a *usage* point of view) on both the receptive and productive levels must become habitual and automatic before they are said to be mastered by the learners.

The adjustment in second or foreign language learning involves:

      a. the acquisition of some altogether new habits, and

      b. the acquisition of some new habits in contrast with (and to replace) older habits pertaining to the native language.

The acquisition of both of these sets of habits means the mastery of the system that constitutes the target language, English.

3. Examples of Segmental Problems

To illustrate the nature of segmental problems in learning English as a second or foreign language, a few examples are given here that are faced by speakers of Arabic, Armenian, French, German, Italian, and Spanish.

Speakers of Arabic will not easily distinguish between the following pairs of contrastive sounds (phonemes) in English: /p/ and /b/, /k/ and /g/, /f/ and /v/, /ou/ and /ɔ/. Of the first three pairs, Arabic has /b/, /k/, and /f/, tending to make learners hear "pin", "goal", and "vine" as "bin", "coal", and "fine" respectively. Both elements of the pair of vowels do not exist in Arabic. Arab learners of English will, therefore, need to develop new habits recognizing the contrasts between the elements of each pair. With reference to /ou/ and /ɔ/, Arabic has neither element. To learn the sets of consonants in contrast, learners must develop new habits to replace the old native habits of hearing the constrastive elements as the same; and to learn the pair of vowels, altogether new habits are to be formed hearing and producing each one separately and also in contrast with each other.

Speakers of Armenian, French, and German have quite a bit of trouble with English /θ/ and /ʃ/. Interestingly, Armenians and most Germans would hear and use /t/ in the place of /θ/ and /d/ in the place of /ʃ/, while speakers of French would hear and substitute /s/ for /θ/ and /z/ for /ʃ/. For example, the words "thin" and "that" would be heard and pronounced as "tin" and "dat" by speakers of Armenian and German, and "sin" and "zat" by French speakers.

Among the phonological problems faced by French and Italian learners of English would be the distinction between the vowels /i:/ and /i/ as in "seat" and "sit". Both French and Italian have the vowel /i:/, but not the contrastive vowel /i/, making their speakers hear and pronounce the words "kin", "fit", "sick", and "lip" as "keen", "feet", "seek", and "leap" respectively.

Speakers of Spanish learning English would have quite a challenge producing initial consonant clusters without using an intrusive vowel first. For example, because in Spanish there is no initial cluster /sp/, native speakers of Spanish would tend to say, "I *e*speak *e*Spanish." It is interesting to observe, with reference to initial, medial, and final clusters in English, how different speakers of other languages handle them. For example, while a Spanish speaker would tend to use a vowel in front of an initial consonant cluster, a speaker of Arabic would find it naturally more convenient to break initial, medial, and final clusters and separate the elements by using a vowel in the middle of the cluster. This way, words like "street", "excuse", and "fourth" may be pronounced, by quite a number of learners, as "s*e*treet", "ex*e*cuse", and "four*e*th".

While a contrastive phonological analysis would indicate, in advance, which particular English sounds present problems to speakers of specific languages, an error analysis in class would provide teachers with the real problems faced and the extent of their seriousness. For example, with reference to the problems mentioned above that speakers of Arabic have, an error analysis would clearly show that /v/ (in contrast with/f/) and /g/ (in contrast with /k/) are much easier to learn and master than /p/ (in contrast with /b/) and /ou/ and /ɔ/ (separately and in contrast with each other).

4. Examples of Supra-Segmental Problems

A few important matters relating to supra-segmental elements are brought up here only to show their significance in learning English.

It would probably be unrealistic to expect speakers of other languages to master the rhythm of English. It would take many years of exposure to native English speech before this can be done with ease and native-like precision. However, if the rhythm of sentences is not mastered at the native-like level, learners of English can still be understood quite well if their word and sentence stresses, as well as their basic intonational patterns, are produced adequately.

Perhaps one of the hardest features of English to master is word stress, primarily because of its high degree of unpredictability. Learners of English whose native languages exhibit some uniformity in their word stress patterns will have enormous problems with English word stress. For example, while this feature does necessarily apply to all words, French speakers would normally use a primary stress on the last syllable of a word. Without the added French phonetic coloration of the consonants and vowels in the following sentence, one would still detect an audible French element if the sentence were to be pronounced with the primary stresses falling on the italicized vowels: At this mom*e*nt, my intent*io*n is to rel*a*te to you a fam*ou*s stor*y* which is found in the ann*a*ls of our histor*y*.

Learners of English whose languages exhibit a very high degree of predictability in the placement of primary, secondary, and weak stresses in their words would naturally color English words with the same stress patterns of their native languages. Arabic is a case in point. For example, if the syllabic structure of a word (any word) in Arabic is cvcvcc (consonant and vowel sequencing), the primary stress would fall on the second syllable in all cases. When learners, therefore, come across such words in English as "didn't", "wasn't", "couldn't", and "shouldn't", they would produce these words in the same way, stresswise, putting the primary stress on the second syllable. For another example, the syllabic pattern cvcvcvcvcv would have the primary stress on the third syllable. When learners of English come across the word "laboratory", the spelling gives them the clue that the syllabic structure is similar, and they pronounce the word with all five vowels, giving the third vowel the strongest stress. It is obviously doubly confusing to some learners to realize that in American English the primary stress falls on the first syllable, the secondary stress falls on the penultimate syllable, and the first "o" is silent, while in British English the primary stress falls on the second syllable, and the second "o" is silent.

Sentence stress in English is usually quite easily mastered on the receptive (understanding) level. On the productive level, however, it is a different story. When speaking or reading, speakers of other languages tend to speak slowly, giving each word its due. As a result, you can easily see why the meaningful contrast between the two following sentences can be confused if the sentences (especially the second) are read with each word given primary stress: *My friend didn't eat the apple. Your friend did.*

Languages that are not tone languages (where pitch is an integral part of the word) use intonational patterns and contours to elicit a variety of meanings: finality, nonfinality, series, surprise, fear, questions, etc. The main problem for learners of English is not the contours themselves but their distribution that may present some confusion.

For example, many languages use a rising pitch at the end of an utterance to signal a question. The tendency for speakers of such languages would be to end every English question with a rising pitch, when most questions in English (especially the ones starting with question words like "where", "what", when", "how", "do", "is", etc.) end with a falling pitch.

Another element related to the distribution of intonational contours can be baffling to learners of English on the receptive (understanding) level. Quite a number of native English speakers use a rising pitch contour in the middle of a sentence as an attention getter; sometimes public speakers use this as a technique to keep their audiences awake. Many learners of English find this terribly confusing because they interpret it as a form of a question; it puts them off so badly that many times they miss the rest of the sentence. An example of such a sentence would be the following, the italicized word indicating where the rising pitch occurs:

> The other day when I went to the *library* I found the article I was looking for.

5. Fluency and Linking Problems

Fluency means the production of speech easily, comfortably, intelligibly, and at normal speed. Some languages (like French), when produced fluently, have a high degree of *linkage* or *liaisoning*. *Linking* means the production of words as though they are connected in the stream of speech to sound like a single word or sentence.

Take a look, for example, at this sentence:

> I'm sitting in an arm chair.

Obviously, if every word is produced separately and independently, one would notice the word boundaries easily and perhaps even the glottal stops at the onset of the words "in", "on", and "arm". At normal speed and with intelligible (at least to native speakers of English) fluency, all the words would be linked together with the elimination of all the glottal stops.

Such fluency and linking features cause ESL/EFL learners varying degrees of comprehension problems. In the beginning stages, clear pronunciation and enunciation may be in order before normal speed and fluency (with linking) are attempted.

Additionally, because sounds influence each other, a good number of consonants and vowels have their qualities changed as a result of their proximity to other sounds. For example, /n/ and /t/ in American English have the same point of articulation: the alveolar ridge. Consequently, at normal speed, the /t/ tends to disappear in such words as "wanted", "panties", and "sentence". Such influences also exist across word boundaries. For example, take these two sentences:

"I'll miss you."/"I'll buzz you."

The point of articulation for /s/ and /z/ is also the alveolar ridge in the words "miss" and "buzz". The point of articulation for /j/ in "you" is the palate. At normal speed, in anticipation of a palatal /j/, both the /s/ and the /z/ in "miss" and "buzz" are articulated a little further back than usual, making them alveopalatal and sounding like /ʃ/ and /ʒ/ respectively. At a slower speed and with clear enunciation, the two sentences would sound: /ail mis ju:/ and /ail bʌz ju:/. At normal speed, they may sound: /ailmiʃju:/ and /ailbʌʒju:/. Sometimes the way a sound may influence another - assimilation-results in a complete absorption of one of them. For example, at normal speed, the sentence "We'll miss Sharon", will sound like /wi:l miʃʃærən/ instead of /wi:l mis ʃærən/ at slower speeds. ESL/EFL learners can easily be putt off by examples like these that abound in fluent native speech.

6. Generative Phonology

Generative Phonology is the name given to a highly specialized approach to the study of the sound system in a language. Its purpose is to prescribe a finite number of phonological rules which will enable a person to *generate* an infinite number of sounds in a language with their native accuracy and in appropriate situations.

For example, all the information presented earlier about the quality and distribution of the English allophones (contoids and vocoids) would be reduced to rules. The rules, as such, would not be known to the layman or the native speaker of the language. The native speaker would normally pronounce (produce) accurate allophones in their appropriate positions naturally. Describing this natural and native production and reducing it to rules is what is involved in generative phonology.

Similarly, all the detailed information about how sounds influence each other would be turned into generative phonological rules. The same would also be true of morpho-phonemic changes as in the case of the regular plural endings /s/, /z/, and /iz/ in such words as "cats", "dogs", and "cages" respectively.

Because of the limited applied value of generative phonology in the classroom, emphasis in this book has been placed on the information and criteria that would be more instrumental in bringing about more effective results in a learning-teaching situation.

Chapter Twelve

The Mastery of English Phonology

1. Introduction

The elements of language (pronunciation, vocabulary, and grammar) must be learned by students on two levels: the receptive level and the productive level. In other words, learning the elements of language means both understanding and using them. The degree of students' receptive ability in language is measured by the speed and correctness with which they understand what they hear and read. And the degree of their productive ability in language is measured by the speed and correctness with which they speak and write. The receptive ability alluded to here is not to be construed as a passive activity; the responses, reaction, and interaction that follow what is heard or read make this receptive ability a very active process.

Speed and correctness can only be reached through practice. This is true of all activities such as eating, driving, typing and playing. And it is also true of hearing and understanding speech, speaking, reading, and writing. In language learning, practice means practice in understanding and using the elements of language. It does not mean practice in knowing and talking *about* these elements.

2. The Importance of Models

Practice requires repetition, and repetition requires the provision of a model. In language teaching and learning situations, it is usually the teacher who provides the live model in class. The provision of models, however, should not be limited to the teacher. Guests in class can provide other models; electronic equipment (such as cassettes, tape recorders, discs, radio and television programs, movies, VCRs, etc.) can bring into the classroom a variety of language models. Naturally, the students' exposure to English outside the classroom, whether at home or in the community, can add much to the varieties and models provided. Repetition may be done in different ways, but one successful method is to have the teacher:

> (a) read all the material (a dialogue, a paragraph, or story) aloud;
> (b) then read each sentence or phrase twice and ask students to repeat once in groups;
> (c) then read each sentence or phrase once and ask students to repeat in groups;
> (d) and finally read each sentence or phrase once and ask students to repeat individually.

3. The Desired Standard of Achievement

The provision of models raises a significant question: What standard of achievement is desired for students of English as a second language? The answer lies in a range that goes from an ideal standard (as the highest possible level of achievement) to a minimum standard (as the lowest acceptable level of achievement). The highest level, in terms of pronunciation, is native-like proficiency. The lowest acceptable level of proficiency in pronunciation is intelligibility (being understood). Between these two levels (the lowest intelligibility level and the highest, native-like level) is a vast range and a long way to go. In second language learning, students cannot hope to surpass the level of proficiency provided by their various models.

4. The Importance of Contrast

In teaching English pronunciation to speakers of other languages, it is important to teach contrasting elements together. For example, in Arabic there is no /p/ phoneme in contrast with a /b/ phoneme as is the case in English. Therefore, it is not only essential for speakers of Arabic to hear and produce /p/ as such, but to hear and produce it in contrast with /b/. This means that speakers of Arabic have learned the English /p/ only when they can recognize it in the speech of others and when they can produce it, in contrast with /b/, in all positions and in consonant clusters. The same, of course, is true for all the other sounds. Two points are to be considered when selecting the contrasting pairs of sounds. The first is the closest sound phonetically (in English) to the sound that is new or foreign to the learner. The second is the sound that learners substitute (in English) for the problem sound; this is often a sound that exists in the learner's native language. For example, many speakers of Arabic produce a phonetic [p] in their colloquial Arabic speech when /b/ (the phoneme) occurs before [s] or [t], turning the voiced [b] to a voiceless [p]. The tendency, then, for speakers of Arabic, is to substitute /b/ for /p/ in English. Also [p] and [b] are very similar (except for the voicing) to each other phonetically in English.

For another example, [θ] and [ʃ] are phonetically very close to each other in English, as are [s] and [z]. French students, who have a phonemic distinction between /s/ and /z/ in French, but no /θ/ or /ʃ/, would tend to substitute /s/ for /θ/ and /z/ for /ʃ/. The /s/-/θ/ contrast and the /z/-/ʃ/ contrast would be significant in the teaching of /θ/ and /ʃ/ to speakers of French.

5. The Importance of Occurrence

Sounds are obviously always in some context: a word, a phrase, a sentence, etc. Where specific sounds occur and what phonetic characteristics they have in different places may be very important - and more so if the aim is to reach a higher level towards native-like speech. The distribution of sounds in a language is interesting. Phonemes will have different allophones (phonetic varieties) occurring in different phonetic environments. The English phoneme /p/, for example, will have [pʰ] occurring in initial position before a vowel and [p] occurring elsewhere (medially and in clusters). English /l/ will have a lighter phonetic variety in initial position and a darker variety in medial and final positions. In Chapters 6 and 7, the consonants and vowels of English were given, along with their phonetic varieties and occurrences.

For speakers of other languages, some phonetic problems (not serious enough to be unintelligible) may arise in their learning of English because of the distribution of different allophones.

6. The Importance of Context

Language does not exist in a vacuum. Any utterance will have to be placed in some context for any person to get its full significance. In this respect, contexts are of two kinds: linguistic contexts and extra-linguistic context. Of these two, linguistic contexts are the larger language forms of which an utterance is only a part. Extra linguistic contexts are the environmental, social, cultural settings in which the utterance is placed. Both of these contexts play a major role in the semantic value of the utterance.

For example, let us consider the meaning of the last sentence in this short paragraph:

The students arrived early in class. Some of them spoke highly of the competitive basketball team, while others strongly defended the home team. A fight ensued, and two students got hurt. *The teacher was in class.*

In such a linguistic context, the meaning of the last sentence goes way beyond its words and structure. It means that the teacher witnessed the whole incident and, to a point at least, negligently allowed the accident to happen.

Now let us take this sentence in isolation linguistically:

The teacher is in class.

The extra-linguistic setting will be of great help in understanding the meaning of the sentence more fully. Here are some different situations which give the above sentence different meanings:

(a) The teacher has been absent for a week and the students were happy without any work to do. The sentence, *The teacher is in class,* now means that the teacher is well again and the students can expect to return to serious work.

(b) The teacher always read the names of the students when he entered the class. But he was usually late to class. So the students stayed in the field for a longer time before coming to class. Today the teacher came on time. The sentence, *The teacher in is class,* now means that the teacher is going to mark most students late and that they are going to suffer the consequences.

(c) The teacher was behind the board where no one saw him. The students thought that he was away and, therefore, made a lot of noise. One student happened to see the teacher and said, *"The teacher is in class."* The sentence now means that everybody should be quiet.

For another example, if we have a sentence like:

We must go back to school now,

what other sentences would be equal in meaning to it? Here are a few:

The teacher is waiting for us.
We are expected there now.
We have been here long enough.

In a particular situation, however, the following sentence would be equal in meaning:

It is half past nine.

The same idea applies in cultural settings. A people's culture includes their customs, traditions, ways of thinking and behaving, and the like. What is done or accepted in a particular situation in a particular culture may not be done or accepted in a similar situation in a different culture. Language, as a conveyor of meanings, will be interpreted differently as a result of different cultural backgrounds. This is why cultural orientation is very important in second or foreign language teaching. Cultural orientation means learning *about* another culture; it does *not* mean copying, adopting, or imposing that culture on learners.

7. Language in Use

Two important competencies are involved in language learning: linguistic competence and communicative competence. Linguistic competence is a person's ability and skills in using the language forms and structures, including, of course, the sounds. Communicative competence goes beyond that; it is the ability to select, from a wide variety of possible forms and structures, what is most appropriate in a very specific situation to convey the desired meaning. On the receptive level, communicative competence means the ability to understand the forms and structures of the language utterances heard or read, and to respond to them appropriately in a given situation. This is language in use.

The communicative approach to language teaching and learning emphasizes the fact that language is a live means of communication and that actual, live, real language use is of the utmost significance. It also insists that language is used to communicate specific notions, functions, and feelings in a variety of situations (formal, informal, serious, playful, etc.) with a variety of people (elders, peers, bosses, casual acquaintances, intimate friends, and the like).

The whole language approach integrates the four language skills as well as the three component parts of language. Learners are to view language as a whole and to attempt to use it in as natural a way as possible with as little inhibition as possible. Themes of interest to the learners are picked in order to make language use and learning relevant and fun at the same time.

These approaches are very practical in the sense that students learn language elements that they immediately experience in use. Combining these two approaches (the communicative approach and the whole language approach) can make language learning very effective and dynamic. However, if both of these approaches are followed without enough attention to structural matters (including, of course, phonological matters), second and foreign language learners may end up learning a few elements that they can probably use here and there without developing the necessary linguistic skills on the basis of which, given their innate abilities, they would be able to generate an unlimited number of language forms. Besides, teachers whose own command of English is not very strong may find these approaches very difficult to adopt and follow, especially if they have not been adequately trained to use them.

Chapter Thirteen

Teaching and Learning English Phonology

1. Introduction

Effective teaching is, to a very high degree, measured in terms of effective learning. The ultimate, as well as immediate, goals and objectives should, therefore, always be seen from the learners' points of view. Even the wording of any objectives should reflect this viewpoint. But no objectives can be effectively achieved if the two other component parts of an educational operation are not adequately planned for: the content of the program and the methodology employed.

This chapter deals precisely with the educational tools required to bring about optimal results in a language classroom.

2. Classroom Control

The success of teachers depends, to a great extent, on their control of the learning-teaching situation. Control here means to be in charge of. If the learning-teaching situation is under control, teachers can direct class activities in such a way as to yield the best results. If possible, then, teachers must be able to:

- control the temperature of the room,
- control ventilation,
- control lighting,
- control the seating arrangement of students,
- control class order, and
- control the instructional part of the situation

The control of temperature, ventilation, and lighting depends very much on what is provided by the physical plant. Teachers with little experience, however, often fall into the trap of not making full use of what the school provides. Proper temperature, ventilation, and lighting are basic requirements for any learning-teaching situation.

The seating arrangement may be done in several ways. Some teachers prefer to seat students according to height, the shortest occupying the front seats and the tallest occupying the rear seats. Other teachers find it best to seat students according to the alphabetical order of their names. Still other teachers use a third method of letting students select their own seats the first day of class. When there is good reason to make a special request for a change, the teachers may agree to make such a change. A very helpful suggestion regarding seating is the preparation of a seating chart for each class. This makes control of the class easier and speeds up the teachers' association with the names and faces of the students. If possible, the seating arrangement should allow for very desirable work in small groups.

The control of class order and discipline is very essential in any classroom situation. In a democracy, teachers aim at developing self-discipline in their students. The development of responsibility and self discipline can only come through proper approaches, good relations, exemplary role modeling, and effective guidance and counseling.

Before problems arise, teachers must try to prevent them. After problems arise, however, teachers must use certain measures in order not to have the act repeated and in order to build further responsibility and self-discipline for the future.

But the most important part of the teachers' work is control of the instructional situation. This control is enhanced by the teachers' systematic and thorough planning.

3. The Unit Plan

Every course is divided into units. Units extend over a period of time and cover a number of lessons. A unit is to be seen as a whole, just as the word unit implies. This unit (this whole) is to consist of a variety of activities that are related to each other in a very meaningful way. All the lessons of the unit are to be seen this way. An effective unit plan would consist of the following component parts:

a. *The unit topic.* This may be thematic in nature and centered around student interests. Examples of themes would be exploring space, home pets, a shopping spree, school sports, caring for older people, etc.

b. *The time period and number of lessons required.*

c. *The general objectives of the unit.* These may be of two kinds: behavioral objectives and affective objectives. Examples of behavioral objectives would be reading a passage in a given time and answering questions about it orally, deciding on the vocabulary to use in the development of a story, conducting a dialogue in class to show enthusiasm and animation, etc. Examples of affective objectives would be to love animals, to appreciate the physical world we live in, to learn the value of money, etc. It is always good to have a combination of both types of objectives. Of course, behavioral objectives would be more easily assessed.

d. *The materials and sources to be used.* This is a list of the actual transparencies, films, books, magazines, handouts, maps, cassettes, flash cards, pictures, or any learning aids to be used in any given unit.

e. *The new terminology, jargon, or vocabulary to be introduced and used in the unit.*

f. *The activities that students will perform in class.* This would be a list of such activities as reading a particular passage, writing answers to some questions, working in pairs or small groups on some class project, acting out a dialogue or excerpts from a text, telling stories, asking each other questions about some activity attended in the community, etc.

g. *Extra-class activities, assignments, and projects.* This would be a list of the actual activities to be performed by students individually or in groups as a means of preparing for class work or as reinforcement for what has been learned in class.

h. *Evaluation vehicles.* This would include the types of activities, performances, tests, etc. that would aid the teachers in assessing the students' success in achieving the objectives of the unit.

4. The Lesson Plan

The preparation of lesson plans is probably the most important part of the teachers' professional work. Lesson plans are prepared on the basis of the unit plan. An individual lesson plan does not only guide teachers' activities in class, but it also gives teachers a sense of direction in the course and helps them to attain, bit by bit, the broader, more general objectives of the unit and, ultimately, the whole course. The essential component parts of a lesson plan are the following:

a. *The subject or subjects of the lesson.* This would naturally be a part of the unit topic.

b. *The specific objectives of the lesson.* Some teachers write the general objectives of the unit first as a reminder of the broader goals. The specific objectives of the lesson should obviously contribute to the achievement of the general unit objectives. If the general unit objectives include both behavioral and affective objectives, it would be expected to have both types among the specific lesson objectives.

c. *The specific materials and sources to be used in teaching the lesson,* including all the learning aids.

d. *The procedure.* This is the longest and most detailed part of the lesson plan. It includes all the review items, all the questions to be asked, all the explanations and presentations to be given, all the learning activities that the students perform in class, and any form of test administered. Some teachers indicate in the margin how long (in minutes) each activity is to take; this is to make sure that the basic parts of the lesson plan are adequately covered in class.

e. *The assignment.* This is to be announced in class at an appropriate time during the class period. The assignment is not to be given only for the sake of having the students *do* something. It should be planned and well thought out. The following are the major characteristics of a good assignment:
- It should be difficult enough to require some hard work and easy enough so that students can do it by themselves.
- It should be a learning experience for them.
- It should be useful and meaningful.
- It should be interesting.
- It should reinforce something they have learned in class.

A lesson plan of course includes all the details of the class period. A very helpful suggestion (particularly for teachers with little or no experience) is to include more material in the lesson plan than they can expect to finish in one period. A short lesson plan might puzzle new teachers towards the end of the class period and leave them with little or nothing to do.

A lesson plan is a means, not an end. It seems important to remind teachers that moving away from a prepared lesson plan may at times be necessary. Very often the students' knowledge is not enough for the learning of a new item in the teacher's plan. At the discovery of such a weakness, the teacher should first turn away from the prepared lesson plan and teach the students the necessary missing items. It is at such moments that the experience and intelligence of a teacher show the most.

f.   *Future orientation.* This is a brief introduction to the next lesson so that students can anticipate what is coming next. If the lesson happens to be the last one in the unit, this orientation would be an introduction to the next unit in anticipation.

g.   *The evaluation.* This is to include the assessment of student achievement as well as teaching effectiveness, resulting in changes in, or new directions for, the following lesson or lessons. This evaluation is usually done after the lesson has been taught.

5. Integrated Lessons

Two important sets of elements need to be integrated meaningfully to make the learning of a second language relevant and effective. The first consists of the component parts of language: phonology, vocabulary, and grammar. Language is a whole, and it should be taught as a whole. To compartmentalize it only helps students to see the bits rather than the whole. Sentences, discourse, stories, reports, dialogues, and all examples of language in use include phrases and sentences, which include words, which in turn include sounds. Sounds permeate words, and words permeate larger linguistic constructions. Pronunciation exercises, whenever they are needed, should be done methodically and in a short space of time. More importantly, they should be seen as part of a whole. This can be accomplished by having the exercises emanate from certain words or passages in the text of the lesson.

The second set to be integrated consists of the four language skills: listening, speaking, reading, and writing. Perhaps listening should also include hearing (the contrastive elements in the second language). All four of these skills can be and should be taught simultaneously. Breaking them down by compartmentalizing them should be reduced to a bare minimum when, and only when, a particular detail is emphasized, be it a matter of comprehension, pronunciation, meaning, or any aspect of writing (spelling, punctuation, sentence structure, paragraphing, etc.). In this regard, two of the latest approaches to language teaching should be used as extensively as possible: whole language (which is thematically based and which integrates all the elements of language) and the communicative approach (which emphasizes language use in appropriate situations). Structural exercises in pronunciation like the ones suggested in the next section (or any other structural exercise in grammar) should be used sparingly when needed; and when they *are* needed, such structural exercises can be extremely instrumental in developing language (as oppose to communicative) competence. Unit and lesson plans should reflect this integrated, whole language approach.

6. Linguistic Pedagogy: Materials and Methods

The focus in this book is on phonology, but it must be remembered that students learn language best when it is presented as a whole. To see the parts in the context of the whole would be much more meaningful. As has been stated earlier, it is language in use (or communicative competence) that is the target. At times, however, it is important to concentrate on bits in order to overcome a particular problem and/or to establish a desired language habit.

Linguistic pedagogy covers the elements of content (the materials to be used) and methodology. Specific examples of materials and methods are suggested here only to illustrate the type of activities that teachers can direct students to perform as a means of establishing proficiency in English phonology.

If Armenian, German, and Scandinavian students, among others, have a problem hearing /θ/ in contrast with /t/, an *exercise* like this one may be helpful:

	/t/	/θ/
In words:	tin	thin
	true	through
	tree	three
	cutting	nothing
	boat	both
In phrases:	to cut a tree	nothing thin

	let him out	north and south
	bright city lights	a thousand things
Combined in sentences:	Little things mean a lot.	
	Thank him for telling the truth.	
	He read *A Thousand and One Nights.*	

Here is an exercise for speakers of French and others who have a problem with /θ/ in contrast with /s/:

	/s/	/θ/
In words:	sing	thing
	sick	thick
	fussing	nothing
	force	fourth
	Norse	north
In phrases:	sing a song	worth nothing
	same voice	three things
	taste some sweets	tenth month
Combined in sentences:	All Sam's horses are healthy and strong.	
	Last Thursday was a nice day.	
	The south is full of nice things.	

For French, Italian, and other learners with a problem distinguishing /i/ from /i:/, this may be helpful:

	/i:/	/i/
In words:	seat	sit
	sheep	ship
	beet	bit
	eat	it
	sleepers	slippers
In phrases:	eat a meal	skip the skit
	even he	bit by bit
	she's a dear	if it's lit
Combined in sentences:	She's feeling fit.	
	Fill it with beef.	
	He licked the sweet.	

In using such exercises, it is often helpful to have *minimal pairs*. A *minimal pair* is a pair of words with a minimal difference in sounds: the sounds of a contrastive pair. For example, for /p/ and /b/, a minimal pair would be "pat" and "bat"; for /k/ and /g/, "coal" and "goal"; and for /i:/ and /i/, "leave" and "live". Of course, it is not always possible to find minimal pairs, especially if a teacher is interested in limiting the vocabulary provided in the exercise to familiar

words. Whether minimal pairs are used or not, it is advisable to have
words or sentences containing the pair of contrastive sounds in different
positions: initially, medially, finally, and in some clusters.   For
example, for /p/ and /b/:   "pat"/"bat", "apple"/"able", "lap"/"lab",
"pray"/"bray", and "harp"/"herb".

Sometimes students are asked to repeat words or phrases in a *mim-
mem* exercise.   *Mim-mem*, as such, is a minimal pair standing for
mimicry and memorization. This can at times, along with rhymes and
songs, be quite helpful in the development of habits and fluency.

To let students *see* that the phonological contrast is truly significant
and meaningful, pictures and charts may be used quite advantageously.
The use of the eyes (along with the ears) can speed up learning and
make it more effective. For example, in teaching pairs of sounds such
as /i/ in contrast with /i:/ and /ou/ in contrast with /ɔ/, it would help to
let the student see the meaningful difference between these sounds in
pictures like:

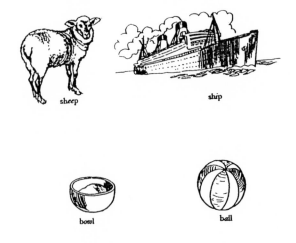

sheep

ship

bowl

ball

The same principle can be applied to the teaching of vocabulary and
grammatical features, especially if there are phonological elements
involved.   For example, in teaching the plural endings, which are

morphological features that are phonologically controlled, one can use pictures like these:

Besides their use in the teaching of linguistic features, pictures and charts may have other uses especially if they are properly selected. They may develop students' artistic sense as well as their interest in reading. They may also develop an understanding of different or foreign cultures which cannot be done as well in class by words alone.

Dramatization is another very helpful device for teaching language elements, especially phonological ones. Dramatization may be an effective supplement to pictures and charts. Dramatization involves action which may be performed by the teacher, the students, or both. This action, besides its educational benefits, creates an active atmosphere in the classroom. Here, as in the case of pictures and charts, a situation is created that is related to the language used. The major difference between pictures and dramatization is that in pictures the situation is still, whereas in dramatization it is dynamic.

One advantage of dramatization over pictures is that very little (if any) materials are needed. On the other hand, however, dramatization requires greater ability on the part of the teacher.

Dramatization may be used in teaching all linguistic features, but its greatest benefits are in the teaching of:
- action words, such as *sit, run, walk, jump, etc.,*
- quality words, such as *fast, slow, big, small,* etc.,
- grammatical words, such as *in* the room, *into* the room, *on,* the table, *under* the chair, etc., and
- expressions where action and the changes in the voice are used together.

It is this last one relating to expressions that cannot be overemphasized for its importance of teaching and learning all the elements of pronunciation, especially the prosodic ones.

Dialogues are extremely instrumental in developing oral proficiency. They simulate real life situations and can be seen by learners as very relevant to their lives and personal experiences. Doing already prepared dialogues or creating real ones in class on the basis of a particular topic or theme would create interest and enthusiasm, which are important motivational devices for learners. Free and open dialogues in class among students are also very helpful.

Reading aloud, which should never be overdone in class, can be very meaningful at times. It is interesting to see how many students in class can understand their colleagues' reading, especially if they are not following the printed text themselves. This can be the test for good reading proficiency.

Listening comprehension is another objective to be attained. Students can be made to listen carefully to their teachers, to their peers (speaking or reading), to recorded passages in class, or to any broadcast, film, etc. Practice and training in these spheres of listening can help develop the learners' comprehension.

7. Testing Student Proficiency in English Phonology

Students' work and progress must be evaluated and measured from time to time in order to reduce waste, to increase the benefit from the teacher's efforts, to direct students' study, and to guide the teacher in the selection of teaching materials and methods. For purposes of evaluation and measurement, proper tests must be prepared and given. A good and complete language test must be designed to test students' ability and skills in pronunciation (segmental and supra-segmental elements in oral speech), vocabulary, grammatical features (morphology and syntax), comprehension, communicative proficiency, and written work (including all aspects of writing).

Either oral or written tests may be given to measure students' skills in English consonants and vowels, particularly the ones that are different from the consonants and vowels in their native language. Oral tests may involve a conversation in which the mastery of particular consonants and vowels is discovered; or they may involve the reading of a passage in which particular consonants and vowels are included. Written tests may involve matching similar sounds. For example, to distinguish between /f/ and /v/ and between /ou/ and /ɔ/ is difficult for Arab students. For these pairs, sentences may be prepared to test the students' ability to distinguish between the sounds. Students, for example, may be asked to draw a circle around the numbers in the right-hand column that represent similar sounds in the left-hand column.

(a) The -ire in the -ort was -ery hot.
        1   2   3 | 1 2 3
(b) P-l likes to r-w a b-t.
        1   2   3 | 1 2 3

Both word stress and sentence stress must be included in a language test. If the test is oral, involving reading or conversation, students' ability to use the proper word and sentence stresses can be discovered by the teacher. If the test is written, students' ability to place primary stress can be tested by asking them to draw a circle around the number in the right-hand column that represents the stressed syllable in the left-hand column.

(a) beautiful
   1 2 3   1 2 3
(b) civilization
   1 23 4 5   1 2 3 4 5
(c) difficulty
   1 2 3 4   1 2 3 4

Since sentence stress depends on a larger context than just the sentence itself, that context must be given too.

(a) John did not see books on the table.
   He saw pens on the table.
   1 2   3   4   1 2 3 4
(b) We are eating cookies.
   What are you eating?
   1 2   3   4   1 2 3 4

Alert teachers can always catch the types of pronunciation errors and problems in their students' pronunciation. It is on this basis that specialized (and short) pronunciation exercises may be prescribed and given to those who need them remedially.

Chapter Fourteen

English Spelling and Pronunciation Correlated

1. Introduction

It does not take long for a learner of English (native or foreign) to realize that spelling presents many problems and challenges. To state it mildly, one of the worst spelled languages in the world is English. Very few learners realize, however, that there are very good reasons for the great varieties and inconsistencies in the correlation between English spelling and pronunciation.

To begin with, the Germanic tribes (the Angles, the Saxons, and the Jutes) first invaded the island in 476 A.D., bringing with them and using a Low Germanic dialectical variety (spoken in the northern lowlands of Germany) that interacted with a variety of dialects spoken on the island, mainly Latin and Celtic.

Secondly, no language has undergone the changes in pronunciation, vocabulary, and grammar to the same extent that English has undergone in its relatively brief history and development.

Thirdly, no language has been influenced by other languages to the same extent that English has. Latin, Celtic, French, Scandinavian, Greek, and Arabic have all had varying degrees of influence on the originally Germanic language that is now English. As a matter of fact, the vast majority of words used in English today are not Anglo-Saxon in origin; some of the most frequently used words, though, are.

Fourthly, when printing was first introduced in England in 1475, the language had already been through two of the three main historical periods in its development - namely, Old English and Middle English. (The third period, Modern English, may itself be divided into Early Modern English and Late Modern English.) By then (1475), English had been written in a variety of ways by different writers, and it took the printed word a considerably long time to bring about some uniformity.

Finally, Noah Webster personally introduced a good number of spelling changes (mainly intended toward greater simplification and consistency) when he introduced his first American English dictionary. Now, of course, students of English around the world are faced with two spelling systems: American English and British English.

A language that is very well spelled - i.e. a language that has a high correlation between spelling and pronunciation - would have one orthographic (written) symbol for each phoneme (contrastive sound unit) in the language. Some languages (eg. Arabic and Spanish) have a much higher correlation in this respect than English.

2. Some Patterned Correlations

The question about possible correlations between spelling and pronunciation is frequently raised. And, of course, there are certain correlations that make it possible to guess, with some degree of accuracy, how to pronounce unknown words. For example, let us consider a few nonsense words and how they might be pronounced: (Capital *C* stands for *Consonant.)*

nonsense word	guessed pronunciations	But what about
"reen"	/ri:n/	"been" (in the U.S.)
"neab"	/ni:b/	"tread" and "heart"
"iCe"	/ai/	"machine"
"aCe"	/ei/	"climate"
"uCe"	/u:/or/ju:/	"feature"
"rone"	/ou/	"done"
"ko"	/ou/	"do"
"roun"	/roun/or/raun/	"soup"
"naid"	/neid/or/naid/	"plaid"
"bot"	/bat/or/bot/	"woman" and "women"

The guessed pronunciations above would work generally, but the fact remains that there will probably be some real example in English that does not fit. While most single and double consonant letters may not normally present too many pronunciational problems, the case is not so with the vowel letters.

3. The Major Problems
When the writing system is compared with the phonological system of English, major problems seem to arise:

a. There are very few prosodic features that are represented in writing: word and sentence stresses are not indicated at all; intonational patterns are non-existent in the writing system; pause is very inadequately represented in the punctuation marks; and rhythm is not marked at all.

b. The vowel sounds, which number 16 (in American English and 21 (in British English) are represented by only five vowel letters in the alphabet, which naturally necessitates a good number of vowel letter combinations, many of which are pronounced in a variety of ways.

c. Three of the consonant letters (namely, *c, q* and *x*) are redundant and superfluous. Besides, many of the consonant letter combinations are pronounced in different ways.

d. Many letters are silent in certain words.

e. A great many sounds in English are variously spelled.

f. A great many letters and combinations of letters are variously pronounced.

4. The Spelling of English Sounds
While this presentation is not meant to be exhaustive, it nevertheless indicates the extent (and seriousness) of the multiplicity of spellings for the same sounds of English.

Sounds	*Spellings*	*Examples*
/p/	p	"put"
	pp	"supper"
	ph	"shepherd"
/t/	t	"ten"
	tt	"sitter"
	th	"thyme"
	ed	"passed"

/k/	k	"key"
	c	"cake
	q	"quote"
	ck	"lick"
	ch	"choir"
	cc	"acclaim"
/b/	b	"bat"
	bb	"rubbing"
/d/	d	"do"
	dd	"muddy"
	ed	"loved"
/g/	g	"rag"
	gg	"bagged"
	gh	"ghost"
	x	"exit"(gz)
/f/	f	"fine"
	ff	"stuffy"
	ph	"phone"
/v/	v	"vine"
	vv	"savvy"
	f	"of"
/θ/	th	"thin"
	tth	"Matthew"
/ʃ/	th	"then"
/s/	s	"see"
	ss	"messy"
	c	"cite"
	sc	"scene"
/z/	z	"quiz"
	zz	"quizzing"
	s	"cars"
	x	"xylophone"
	ss	"scissors"
/ʃ/	sh	"shine"
	s	"mansion"
	ss	"mission"
	t	"nation"
/ʒ/	s	"measure"
	z	"azure"
/tʃ/	ch	"chin"

	tch	"match"
	c	"cello"
/dʒ/	j	"joy"
	dg	"fudge"
	g	"George"
/h/	h	"ham"
/m/	m	"my"
	mm	"humming"
	mn	"hymn"
	lm	"calm"
/n/	n	"no"
	nn	"banner"
/ŋ/	ng	"ring"
	n	"sink"
/l/	l	"low"
	ll	"follow"
/r/	r	"run"
	rr	"merry"
	l	"colonel"
	wr	"write"
	rh	"rhythm"
	rrh	"myrrh"
/w/	w	"wet"
	o	"doer"(/uw/)
/j/	y	"yet"

/iː/	ee	"need"
	ea	"meat"
	eCe	"mete"
	ei	"receive"
	ie	"believe"
	iCe	"machine"
	ey	"key"
	uay	"quay"
	eo	"people"
	oe	"phoenix"
	e	"me"
	ae	"alumnae"
	y	"happy"

/i/	i	"kid"
	ee	"been"
	ie	"sieve"
	o	"women"
	e	"pretty"
/ei/	aCe	"fame"
	ai	"paid"
	ay	"say"
	ey	"obey"
	eigh	"eight"
	ei	"rein"
	eig	"reign"
/e/	e	"net"
	ea	"thread"
	ai	"said"
/æ/	a	"hat"
	ai	"plaid"
/a/	a	"father"
	ea	"heart"
	o	"cot"
/ə/	e	"paper"
	ai	"mountain"
	i	"pencil"
	aCe	"climate"
	o	"rigor"
	uCe	"vulture"
	no letter	"little"
/ʌ/	u	"hub"
	ou	"enough"
	oCe	"come"
	oo	"blood"
	o	"son"
/ə:/	ea	"heard"
	e	"herd"
	i	"sir"
	y	"myrrh"
	o	"worth"
	u	"disturb"
/u:/	oo	"pool"
	ou	"soup"

	u	"flu"
	ue	"blue"
	uCe	"rude"
	ew	"chew"
	eu	"feud"(/ju:/)
	ui	"suit"
/u/	u	"put"
	oo	"foot"
	o	"woman"
	ou	"could"
/ou/	o	"no"
	ew	"sew"
	oCe	"note"
	owe	"owe"
	ow	"known"
/ɔ/	au	"fault"
	augh	"naught"
	a	"all"
	ou	"four"
	o	"nor"
	oo	"door"
	aw	"raw"
/ai/	i	"alumni"
	eigh	"height"
	y	"my"
	igh	"high"
	ye	"bye"
	uy	"buy"
	iCe	"hide"
	ie	"pied"
/au/	ow	"now"
	ou	"proud"
	ough	"bough"

5. The Pronunciation of English Letters

While this presentation is not meant to be exhaustive, it nevertheless indicates the extent (and seriousness) of the multiplicity of pronunciations for the same letters or combinations of letters in English.

Spellings	Pronunciations	Examples
a	/æ/	"hat"
	/a/	"father"
	/ə/	"alumna"
aCe	/ei/	"rate"
	/ə/	"ultimate"
ae	/i:/	"alumnae"
ai	/ei/	"paid"
	/e/	"said"
	/æ/	"plaid"
	/eə/	"pair"
c	/s/	"cite"
	/k/	"cat"
	/tʃ/	"cello"
ch	/tʃ/	"chin"
	/k/	"choir"
	/ʃ/	"machine"
cq	/k/	"acquire"
e	/i:/	"me"
	/e/	"met"
ea	/i:/	"meat"
	/e/	"head"
	/a/	"heart"
	/ə:/	"heard"
	/iæ/	"beatitude"
	/ijə/	"theater"
eau	/ou/	"beau"
	/ju:/	"beautiful"
gh	/f/	"enough"
	/g/	"ghost"
i	/ai/	"alumni"
	/i/	"sit"
iCe	/ai/	"site"
	/i:/	"machine"
	/i/	"composite"
iu	/jə/	"radius"
o	/a/	"cot"
	/ɔ/	"for"
oa	/ou/	"coat"

oo	/uː/	"pool"
	/u/	"foot"
	/ʌ/	"blood"
	/ouə/	"cooperate"
	/ɔ/	"door"
ou	/uː/	"soup"
	/au/	"proud"
	/u/	"could"
ough	/uː/	"through"
	/ou/	"though"
	/au/	"bough"
	/ʌf/	"enough"
	/ə/	"thorough"
s	/s/	"sing"
	/ʃ/	"mansion"
	/z/	"cabs"
sc	/s/	"scissors"
	/sk/	"scam"
	/ʃ/	"conscious"
sch	/sk/	"school"
	/ʃ/	"schedule"(British)
th	/θ/	"thin"
	/ʃ/	"then"
	/t/	"thyme"
u	/uː/	"flu"
	/u/	"put"
	/ʌ/	"cub"
ue	/uː/	"blue"
ui	/uː/	"suit"
	/uwi/	"fluid"
	/wi/	"conduit"
x	/ks/	"ax"
	/gz/	"exam"
	/z/	"xylophone"
xc	/ks/	"except"
y	/j/	"yes"
	/ai/	"sky"
	/iː/	"lily"

6. Silent Letters

Quite a number of letters are silent in certain words. Examples:

Letters	Examples	Letters	Examples
b	"lamb"	e	"rate"
gh	"though"	h	"oh"
e	"suite"	l	"calm"
n	"hymn"	o	"laboratory"
p	"psyche"	q	"acquaint"
t	"Matthew"	w	"write"

7. Homophonous Words

Several sets of words may be spelled in different ways but pronounced similarly. Examples: reed/read, rite/right/write, deer/dear, wet/whet, see/sea, rein/rain/reign, prey/pray, ate/eight, sine/sign, coat/quote, site/sight, so/sew/sow, doe/dough, hi/high, bear/bare, fair/fare, brake/break, bred/bread, by/bye/buy, air/heir, feat/feet, etc.

Conversely, there are several sets of words that are spelled in the same way but pronounced differently, depending on the context and meaning. Examples: read(/riːd/ and /red/), perfect (/pəːrfəkt/ adjective and /pərfekt/ verb), tear (tiːr/ and teər/), row (/rou/ and /rau/), bow (/bou/ and /bau/), wound (/wuːnd/ and /waund/), etc.

8. Conclusion

Because of the very low correlation between spelling and pronunciation in English, some conclusions are inevitable:

a.   Learning the names of the letters of the alphabet helps only in spelling words aloud and looking up words in reference books, but not so much in pronunciation.

b.   The usefulness of phonics has its limitations.

c.   The greatest help to ESL/EFL learners in this respect comes from exposure to oral English, extensive reading, and practice in writing.

Study Questions

1. Explain the following terms and give an example or two of each:

phonetics	phoneme
articulatory phonetics	phone
acoustic phonetics	allophone
auditory phonetics	segmental element
hard palate	supra-segmental element
soft palate	cluster
voiced sounds	initial position
voiceless sounds	medial position
alveolar ridge	final position
nasalization	length
fricative	stress
affricate	intonation
bilabial	pause
labio-dental	juncture
inter-dental	rhythm
dental	aspirated
glottal	unaspirated
retroflex	assimilation

2. Transcribe the following sentences *phonemically* the way *you* pronounce them:

magnate	magnet	deliver	update
few	call	treasure	ached
barrel	student	matching	whether
fudge	hover	snowy	stirfry
yellowfish	bath	singer	bank

3. Transcribe the following sentences *phonetically* the way *you* pronounce them:

a. I'm sure he can do it.
b. Why all this fuss for nothing?
c. My brothers and sisters have just arrived.
d. When is the last train leaving for New York?

4. Give two examples to show that a change in the sentence stress in each of the sentences in #3 above can give different additional and/or contrastive meanings.

5. What do we mean when we say that word stress in English is unpredictable? Give examples.

6. How can we use intonation to give additional and/or contrastive meanings in English? Give examples.

7. How has this book helped you to become a more effective teacher of English as a second language? In answering this question, refer, among other things, to the following criteria:
a. "sharpening" your ears,
b. ability to control parts of your vocal apparatus,
c. sensitivity to the importance of sounds in language,
d. knowledge about the function of sounds in language,
e. the importance of contrastive (comparative) studies, and
f. the ability to construct exercises for learners of English as a second language.

8. Draw a diagram of the vocal apparatus and name the various parts of it. Then give different examples of sounds that can be produced at different points of articulation.

9. Give examples in English of words that contain sounds of various *types* of articulation and various *points* of articulation.

10. How can your knowledge of articulatory phonetics help you in teaching pronunciation? Illustrate your answer.

11. Why and how is a phonemic analysis important to the linguist and the language teacher?

12. Give a phonetic description of the *initial* and *final sounds* in the following words:
laugh, key, jumping, then, plough, race, dish, thought, chew, big.

13. Give two examples of each of the following:
    (a) a three-syllable word with the primary stress on the first syllable,
    (b) a three-syllable word with a secondary stress,
    (c) a two-syllable word with the primary stress on the second syllable, and
    (d) a two-syllable word with the primary stress on the first syllable.

14. Read the following sentences and mark their intonational contours as you say them. (The information in parenthesis should help you understand the context and situation of the original sentence.)
    (a) Our neighbor's a doctor. (He isn't a lawyer.)
    (b) I have a pen, a pencil, and a ruler. (I have nothing else.)
    (c) Excuse me. (This is said to some people blocking your way.)
    (d) It's a cold day. (This is said to a person as a suggestion to wear something warm.)
    (e) It's a cold day? (Question)
    (f) Someone has arrived. (And he is waiting outside.)
        Who? (Meaning 'Who came?')
    (g) Henry has arrived. (As a news item.)
        Who? (Meaning 'I didn't catch the name'.)
        Henry. (As a clarification.)

15. Why is it better to integrate language lessons?

16. In what way can Phonics help ESL learners? What are some of the limitations of Phonics?

17. Prepare an integrated English lesson (as part of a unit) and include in it an exercise to teach any contrastive pair of English sounds.

18. How would you handle a situation in class where some students pronounced words in a British English way?

19. What is your opinion about the concept of *intelligibility* and the concept of *native-like speech* when it comes to your own students'pronunciation? What are some of the practical steps and activities you would prescribe to implement your opinion?

20. As an ESL teacher, you know how important it is for your students to learn English. What, in your opinion, is the importance or value, for a native speaker of English, to learn a second or foreign language?

Glossary of Technical Terms

accent
The way people speak; a mark indicating vowel quality; a mark indicating stress.

acoustic
Related to sounds.

acoustics
The study of sounds as they go through the air.

affricate
A cluster of two consonants consisting of a stop followed by a fricative; a type of sound articulation.

allophone
A phonetic variety (or non-contrastive phone) of a phoneme.

alveolar
A sound produced with the tongue tip at the alveolar (tooth) ridge; a point of articulation at that position.

alveo-palatal
A sound produced with the tongue between the alveolar (tooth) ridge and the palate; a point of articulation at that position.

articulation
The production of speech sounds

articulatory
Related to the production of speech sounds.

aspirated
A sound produced with a puff of air.

aural
Related to hearing.

bilabial
A speech sound produced with both lips; a point of articulation at that position.

bilingualism
The use of two languages (especially from infancy).

cavity, nasal
The empty space in the nose and nasal passage.

comparative linguistics
See *contrastive linguistics.*

complementary
Making complete.

consonant
A type of speech sound that is produced by having the air stopped temporarily or cause some friction or interruption as it goes through the vocal apparatus; not a vowel; a phoneme of this kind; a letter of this kind.

context
The setting of something: a sound, a word, or a group of words.

contextual
Related to the setting.

contoid
An allophone of a consonant phoneme.

contour
See *intonational contour.*

contrast (n.)
Comparison to see the differences.

contrastive linguistics
The study of language forms compared and contrasted with each other - especially of two different languages.

cords, vocal
The two thick muscles that look like a pair of curtains located at the throat; when they vibrate, they cause voicing; they cause higher pitches of voice when tightened.

dental
A speech sound produced with the tongue tip at or near the upper front teeth; a point of articulation at that position.

dialect
One of several varieties of language spoken by a group of people; the varieties may apply to sounds, words, or grammatical forms.

eme
The concept of contrastiveness, which may apply to language or any other part of human experience.

emic
Contrastive.

etic
Non-contrastive.

final position
A position at the end (of a word or utterance).

first language
The language that children learn first; it is usually their native language.

flap
A speech sound (like [r]) produced by having the tongue tip hit against the alveolar ridge.

fricative
A speech sound produced by having the air cause friction at some point of articulation as it goes through the vocal apparatus; a type of sound articulation.

generate
To produce; to come out with.

generative
Related to the production of something: sounds, words, or utterances.

glide
A move from one sound or pitch level to another.

glottal
Related to the glottis; a point of articulation at that position.

glottis
The empty area separating the vocal cords.

grammar
The (study of the) forms of words (morphology) and order of words (syntax) in a language; the rules which describe these.

grammatical
Related to grammar.

grapheme
A significant or contrastive written form.

homophonous
Sounding the same but with different spellings and meaning.

inflection
The changes in the forms of words (morphology); a change in the pitch of the voice.

initial position
A position at the beginning (of a word or utterance).

inter-dental
A speech sound produced with the tongue tip between (or close to) the upper and lower teeth; a point of articulation at that position.

interference
Something that comes in the way of a smooth flow of an activity.

intonation
The change in the pitch of voice.

intonational contour
A single pattern of pitch change in an utterance.

juncture
The smallest pause or space between words or parts of words.

labial
A speech sound produced at or with both lips; a point of articulation at that position.

labio-dental
A speech sound produced with the upper teeth touching or nearly touching the lower lip; a point of articulation at that position.

larynx
The part of the throat where the vocal cords are located.

lateral
On the side; a point of articulation with the air going out of the mouth at the sides of the tongue; a type of sound articulation.

lexical
Related to words.

linguist
A language scientist; a person who knows about language or can speak a number of them.

linguistic
Related to language or to the study of language.

linguistics
The scientific study of language or anything related to language.

medial position
A position in the middle (of a word or utterance).

mid
Related to the middle.

morpheme
The smallest meaningful segment in a language; a *free morpheme* (like "cat") can stand by itself; a *bound morpheme* must be attached (like the "s" in "cats").

nasal
Related to the nose; a type of sound articulation. See *cavity* also.

nasalization
The production of speech sounds with the air (or part of it) going through the nose.

neurological
Related to the nerves or the nervous system.

neuro-psychological
Related to the nerves and general feelings.

neuro-psycho-physiological
Related to the nerves, the feelings, and parts of the body.

occurrence
Happening; where something (a sound, etc.) takes place.

oral
Spoken aloud.

orthographical
Related to spelling or the writing system.

palatal
A speech sound produced by having the tongue mid touch or nearly touch the palate; a point of articulation at that position.

palate
The part of the roof of the mouth between the alveolar ridge and the velum.

pause
A break or a stop.

pedagogical
Related to the methods of teaching.

phone
A speech sound; any variety of speech sounds.

phoneme
A contrastive sound unit in a particular language.

phonemic
Related to phonemes; contrastive in sound; significant in contributing to meaningful distinctions.

phonetic
Related to phones.

phonetician
A scientist who studies speech sounds or phonetics.

phonetics
The science of speech sounds.

phonological
Related to phonology.

phonology
The study of speech sounds; phonetics and phonemics; the system of speech sounds in a particular language.

physical
Related to the body or to a part of nature.

physiological
  Related to physiology.

physiology
  The science dealing with how parts of the body work.

pitch
  A musical note; a musical note in speech.

plosive
  A speech sound that is produced by having the air stopped before it is released.

primary stress
  The strongest force of breath in speech.

pronounce
  To utter a sound or sounds in speech.

pronunciation
  The way in which sounds are produced in a language.

prosodic
  Related to stress, intonation, pause, juncture, and rhythm in language.

retroflex
  A speech sound produced by having the tongue tip curl upwards and backwards; a point of articulation at that position.

rhythm
  The beat; the beat in language produced by a combination of its prosodic features.

ridge (alveolar, tooth)
  The bumpy part of the roof of the mouth just behind the upper front teeth.

secondary stress
  The second strongest force of breath in speech.

second language

The language people learn after their native language to use in every day communication.

segmental sounds

The consonant and vowel sounds in a language.

semantic

Related to meaning (semantics) in language.

semantics

The study of meaning in language.

semiotic

Related to semiotics.

semiotics

The study of facial expressions and body movements as means of communication.

semi-vowel

A speech sound that is considered partly as a consonant (in terms of structure and behavior) and partly as a vowel (in terms of quality); a type of sound articulation.

sibilant

An alveolar fricative or affricate; a type of sound articulation.

sound segment

See *segmental sounds*

standard

The name given to the dialect in a language that is spoken by educated people in positions.

stop

A speech sound that is produced by having the air stopped somewhere in the vocal apparatus before it is released; a plosive; a type of sound articulation.

stress
The relative force of breath in the production of speech sounds.

submember
A variety; a member of a unit.

supra-segmental sounds
Stress, intonation, pause, juncture, and rhythm in language; the prosodic features of a language; the speech sounds that are not consonants or vowels; the segmental and the supra-segmental sounds in a language make up its phonology.

syllabic
Related to syllables.

syllable
A speech utterance (word or part of a word) that contains a vowel or a syllabic consonant.

syntactic
Related to syntax or word order.

syntax
The order of words in utterances (phrases or sentences).

target language
The second or foreign language to be learned.

tertiary stress
The third strongest force of breath in speech.

tone language
A language (like Chinese) that uses a variety of pitches as an integral part of words to elicit different meanings.

trill
A speech sound that is produced by having the tongue tip flap twice or three times against the alveolar ridge; a type of sound articulation.

unit
A bundle or whole consisting of parts, elements, or varieties.

utterance
A speech production consisting of a sound, a group of sounds, a word, a phrase, or a sentence.

uvula
The small part that hangs down at the back of the mouth.

uvular
A speech sound produced with the back of the tongue touching or nearly touching the uvula; a point of articulation at that position.

velar
A speech sound produced by having the back of the tongue touch or nearly touch the soft part of the roof of the mouth; a point of articulation at that position.

velum
The soft part at the back of the roof of the mouth.

vibrant
A speech sound produced with considerable vibration; a type of sound articulation.

vibrate
To move with a sort of a shake.

vibration
A movement with some shaking.

vocabulary
Words; lexicon.

vocal
Oral.

vocal cords
See *cords*.

voiced (voicing)
A speech sound produced while the vocal cords are vibrating.

voiceless
A speech sound produced while the vocal cords are not vibrating.

vocoid
An allophone or a phonetic variety of a vowel phoneme.

vowel
A type of speech sound that forms a syllable; a speech sound that is produced without any stoppage of the air or major friction or interruption as the air goes through the vocal apparatus; not a consonant; a phoneme of this kind; a letter of this kind.

weak stress
The weakest force of breath in speech.

Selected Bibliographical References

Celvee-Murcia, Marianne (Ed.), *Teaching English as a Second or Foreign Language*, (Second Edition), Heinle and Heinle Publishers, Boston, MA, 1991.

Clark, John and Colin Yallop, *An Introduction to Phonetics and Phonology*, (Second Edition), Blackwell, Cambridge, MA, 1995.

Cox, Carole, *Teaching Language Arts: A Students and Response-Centered Classroom*, (Second Edition), Allyn and Bacon, Needham Heights, MA, 1996.

Froese, Victor (Ed.), *Whole Language Practice and Theory*, (Second Edition), Allyn and Bacon, Needham Heights, MA, 1996.

Gimson, A.C., *An Introduction to the Pronunciation of English*, (Third Edition), Edward Arnold (Publishers) Ltd., London, England, 1980.

Kreidler, Charles W., *The Pronunciation of English: A Course Book in Phonology*, Basil Blackwell, Inc., New York, NY, 1989.

Lado, Robert, *Language Teaching: A Scientific Approach*, McGraw-Hill, New York, NY, 1964.

Lado, Robert, *Language Testing*, Longmans, Green and Co., Ltd., London, England, 1961.

Lado, Robert, *Linguistics Across Cultures*, University of Michigan Press, Ann Arbor, MI, 1957.

Lado, Robert, *Teaching English Across Cultures*, McGraw-Hill, New York, NY, 1988.

Nasr, Raja T., *Whole Education: A New Direction to Fill the Relevance Gap*, University Press of America, Lanham, MD, 1994.

Pike, Kenneth, L., *Language in Relation to a Unified Theory of the Structure of Human Behavior*, Mouton and Co., The Hague, Holland, 1967.

Widdowson, G. G., *Teaching Language as Communication*, Oxford University Press, Oxford, England, 1978.

Wilkins, D.A., *Linguistics in Language Teaching*, Edward Arnold, London, England, 1972.

Wilkins, D.A., *Notional Syllabuses*, Oxford University Press, Oxford, England, 1976.

Wilkins, D.A., *Second Language Learning and Teaching*, Edward Arnold, London, England, 1974.

Index